Open Intelligence:

Changing the Definition of Human Identity

Texts and Talks from the Balanced View Center,
Skåne, Sweden, July 2010

By

The Balanced View Team

Third Edition 2012
Balanced View Media: Mill Valley, California USA 2012

ISBN: 978-0-9886659-0-3

Open Intelligence:
Changing the Definition of Human Identity

TABLE OF CONTENTS

Editor's Introduction v

1. The Beneficial Qualities and Activities of Open Intelligence: The Core of Real Relationship 1

2. Empowering Human Society 25

3. Potent Qualities and Activities of Human Society 49

4. Key Instructions in Beneficial Open Intelligence 68

5. The Mutual Power of Open Intelligence 85

6. Death and Other Afflictive Data 105

7. The Blast that Blows Open the Here-and-Now 120

8. Blowing Open Pleasure 132

9. Potency 148

10. Open Intelligence Society 173

11. The Ferocity of Open Intelligence 190

12. Complete Identity 203

Balanced View Resources 224

EDITOR'S INTRODUCTION

There are times in our lives when we are alerted to previously unseen things that, once seen clearly, are extraordinarily significant and meaningful for us. When we have the recognition, "Wow, life looks very different now," there is often an accompanying feeling that something has shifted in our lives and in the way we see the world. While we should not overestimate or exaggerate events and experiences and give them significance they do not have, at the same time we are greatly benefitted if we are attentive to the times when something has truly changed in our lives.

During a twelve-day period in July 2010, a group of 140 people gathered together at the Balanced View Center in Skåne, Sweden to take part in the Human Identity Summit. For the people who were present at that gathering and for many others who participated online, there was definitely a feeling that something very momentous had occurred and that their vision of the world had indeed shifted. If the intention in the retreat was to explore the true nature of the human identity and to empower people in its most potent expression, then one could surely say that this intention was realized.

The guidance for that exploration came from the talks and texts lovingly provided by the founder of the Balanced View Training, Candice O'Denver. There was a wonderfully reciprocal relationship in the setting where Candice would give of herself completely, and the participants would enthusiastically receive and then give back in equal measure. One could say that it was a form of "call and response," in the sense that Candice would speak skillfully and with great insight for the benefit of the people present, and the participants would respond with their own insight in the form of their powerful value letters at the conclusion of each day's training.

It was clear from the outset that many, many people would benefit if the talks and texts from this powerful retreat were collected into book form. The resulting book that you have before you—*Open Intelligence: Changing the Definition of Human*

Identity—is organized and presented in such a way as to awaken the same sense of insight and discovery that was present in the retreat.

Each of the twelve days of the retreat began with a written text. Candice did not write the texts long in advance; rather, each night she would sit down, consider what the participants needed, and on that basis she would write out the text for the following day. That spontaneous responsiveness and sensitivity is clearly evident in the texts and talks.

On certain days Candice would give a commentary on the written text, and for those days the commentary is included right along with the written text. Each day she would give a talk, which might be based on the text, or it might be based on the needs of the moment. Then in the afternoons the participants would share their value letters, which are their heartfelt reply to the training that day. For the first time in a Balanced View book, some of the value letters have been included, and most happily so, as they provide an extremely powerful response to the "call" that Candice gave in each day's text and talk.

Especially for a reader who is new to the Balanced View Training, it would be important to define the most significant words that are used in the text. The most important term is *open intelligence,* which is used frequently throughout the book. *Awareness* and *clarity* were terms that were used frequently in previous books, and now this very direct and explicit term, *open intelligence*, is being employed in the same way. The meaning of this term is essentially the same as clarity or awareness, but it even more clearly points to our expansive but yet readily accessible natural wisdom. Other terms in the book that refer to the same essence pointed to by open intelligence include *the basic state, natural perfection, our own nature, the great luminosity, super-intelligence, natural intelligence* and *the view.*

The fundamental practice that is discussed throughout the book is that of *relying on open intelligence.* Relying on open intelligence is the core principle of basing one's experience in open intelligence rather than on the passing phenomena.

The phrase *short moments, many times until it becomes obvious* is used to convey the fact that one can rely on open intelligence in each and every moment, and one can continue returning to it for short moments over and over again until the practice becomes naturally spontaneous and continuous.

The term *data* refers to all thoughts, emotions, sensations and experiences that appear in open intelligence. Data might also at times be referred to as *points of view* or *viewpoints*. The key to understanding data/points of view is to see that they have no independent nature and are nothing other than the dynamic reflective energy of open intelligence. The two are inseparable like the color blue and the sky.

Balanced View's Four Mainstays is a system of instruction which came about by participants from all continents asking the questions 'what are we?', 'what is our identity?', 'how can we be of widespread collective benefit?', 'what are our strengths, gifts and talents and how can we share them with each other?'. The Four Mainstays are the themes of this book. The Four Mainstays are: 1) short moments of open intelligence, 2) the trainer, 3) the training and the training media, and 4) the worldwide community. *Open Intelligence Now* is a booklet, which supplements this book and serves as an introduction.

The material for this book was collected, transcribed, proofread and edited by a dedicated team of volunteers. We would like to most graciously thank Candice for this marvelous training given in the Human Identity Summit and also the many volunteers who made this book possible.

The Editors
April 2011
Skåne, Sweden

Day One

THE BENEFICIAL QUALITIES AND ACTIVITIES OF OPEN INTELLIGENCE: THE CORE OF REAL RELATIONSHIP

The Written Text

Your very own open intelligence is naturally endowed with powerful qualities and activities. Open intelligence is the basis and foundation for a totally fulfilling life. It is the very potent, extremely skilled identity that contains all knowledge with nothing left out.

In the first moment of open intelligence, we recognize its tremendous stability, its tremendous potential. We realize we have found our true identity. This realization becomes increasingly vivid.

Open intelligence is necessary, as it provides a completely stable foundation for each moment of everyday life and the capacity to proceed with tremendous power and force. Open intelligence requires 100% commitment and being willing to go to any lengths.

Open intelligence does not deal with superficial aspects of identity but with its innate potency, its actual ability to create radical change.

Short moments of open intelligence are necessary so that we can begin to understand what it is all about. In brief moments of uncontrived open intelligence, we begin to see that open intelligence is the basis of all of our thoughts, seamlessly blended with data. We instinctively recognize the impossibility of separating open intelligence from data in order to achieve some kind of special state.

Identity and relationship based on data always work through name tags in a process of judging this against that. Relying on data literally divides everything up and depletes our energy instead of unifying it in the mutual force of open intelligence.

We really need to see very clearly the disadvantages of maintaining our data streams about identity and relationship. Then we need to extract the power from all data by relying on their open intelligence.

By relying on short moments of open intelligence, we see its real power. With the very real power of each moment of open intelligence, we empower ourselves like an ocean gathers all of its force from single drops of water.

Short moments also allow us to train into a mass of human power, the likes of which are unimaginable. Short moments are very powerful, very radical and very direct. Precise open intelligence, moment to moment, changes human society forever.

In short moments we begin to relate its actual power and purpose to our ordinary everyday life. We recognize that it has always been the infrastructure of our entire life. Even though we did not learn about open intelligence in the past, it has been present and totally powerful all along.

Within our very own open intelligence, we discover that we already have certain qualities: it is self-affirming, and it provides the qualities of relief and power immediately in our own direct experience. This is very convincing and very authoritative. We begin to see that the relief and power of open intelligence are reliable and consistent. We can count on them without fail.

This process is very natural. In open intelligence all of our ups and downs become a single power. The qualities and activities of open intelligence are obvious from the first moment—total relief and total unending power. We cannot reject our real empowered identity and try to be something else.

Open intelligence is the only potential we have, and when we instinctively recognize this, we see that we can use open intelligence powerfully and beneficially in each aspect of living daily life. Open intelligence is extraordinarily special and extremely real and personal. It seals the powerful bond of human society in mutuality and potency. This is real relationship, and we see it clearly and directly.

Open intelligence instantaneously shows how to relate to our own ordinary existence or daily situation as well as to our societal goals. In open intelligence we relate with the details of our everyday life according to our own particular makeup. It is a real and personal experience. And in order to relate to our lives in a clear fashion, there are certain fruits of open intelligence we have to understand. These qualities and activities have a working vocabulary of potency and prosperity. We become fluent in this potent, prosperous vocabulary of body, speech and mind. We are introduced to our basic identity and begin to be able to completely rely on ourselves, perhaps for the first time.

Open intelligence extends in the same way that space extends our sense of ourselves. Its openness expands our definition of identity into a powerful expanse. Open intelligence is everyone's fundamental style, the intrinsic perspective or stance and the way of perceiving the world and working with it. Open intelligence is our most potent and prosperous intelligence.

"Open intelligence" means conciseness and indestructibility are built in. Open intelligence thoroughly cuts the root of reactive mental and emotional tendencies and represents the open awareness of many possible perspectives. Open intelligence corrects or remedies any distortion in a precise and sharp way. Open intelligence is the view pervading all data and sees them clearly.

Open intelligence is penetrating and very personal and very relational. It is very vivid and lucid. Open intelligence knows how to evaluate logically the arguments that are used to explain experience. It can tell whether logic is true or false. It has a sense of constant openness and perspective. For instance, open intelligence is like a flawless crystal ball viewing all of its reflections from hundreds of perspectives, according to where it was placed, the way it was perceived, the distance from which it was looking at it, and so forth.

Open intelligence is not just encyclopedic; it is concise, direct and aware of perspectives from *within* the perspective itself.

Open intelligence takes all perspectives and clearly sees all their aspects. Such indestructibility, conciseness and intimacy with everything is very personal and very real. This is true relationship.

Through the power of open intelligence, human society has an indestructible relationship, potency and skillfulness that have never existed before. We are able to enjoy this power and skill right now, together.

Day One Talk

I want to begin the Human Identity Summit by speaking about relationship and about the Four Mainstays as the basis of open intelligence practice. To practice open intelligence without the Four Mainstays won't be very effective; the Four Mainstays are really required. For open intelligence to become fully juiced up and powerful—just like it always already is—it requires being in intensive relationship with others who are committed to open intelligence as well. This is very simple, very radical and very effective. Once the introduction to open intelligence takes place, then it is a matter of practicing short moments of open intelligence in everyday life and of having a relationship with community—other people who are committed to the same thing.

It is also about having a full-on relationship with a trainer, another person just like you who has made the 100% commitment to open intelligence and is willing to go to any lengths. Why is that relationship important? Because they've been there, so to speak. There are many pitfalls that will be avoided through that relationship.

Additionally, the relationship with the trainer pulls your covers! Let's say you're in bed asleep, all cozied up in your data streams. The trainer pulls your covers. This can only happen in community; without community it might be easy to go off in all kinds of ways, believing that you are really enjoying open intelligence but not ever really totally clear about whether you are or not.

This incredible relationship that people allow themselves to have by coming into community with others in a direct open way is the most empowering relationship they can ever have in life. This is really the most fulfilling, satisfying, pleasureful relationship that can ever be had in life, because it allows for direct, naked encounter—naked in the real sense of being willing to be completely real and not getting detoured into any tunnel of data like thoughts, emotions, sensations or other experiences.

In the practice of open intelligence it's easy to see how these detours have been made: being overly intellectualized, overly emotionalized or overly driven by the senses. This is the core, this is the heart essence of open intelligence. This is why it is absolutely essential to practice open intelligence in relation with community. The power of open intelligence naturally reveals itself in a way that is so much more profound than anything we could have conceptualized in advance.

THE INTRODUCTION TO OPEN INTELLIGENCE

The moment of the introduction of open intelligence is so powerful; it's so engaging, it's so turned on, it's so real, it's so authentic, it's so convincing, and that introduction is unending. Open intelligence is already present; however, we just didn't know it before. Once we know it, there's a process of familiarization and of getting acquainted with its real power. We are getting acquainted with our own power and what we're really capable of in the world. We are able to see clearly without confusion and without any foolish errors one way or another. This is just what we are made of.

Even if human society has existed up till this point without a massive infusion of open intelligence, *with* a massive infusion the whole way of being human changes. It changes, because everyone is clear, direct and present. Everyone is able to engage directly and powerfully, rather than from one of the tunnels of data: too much intellect, too much emotion, being too much driven by the senses.

We each have our own particular thing; I know that in my own life I tended to be very intellectually-oriented and I saw emotions as kind of an unnecessary detour. I thought that to go too far emotionally one way or another never really led anywhere, so it was better to stay intellectually on track. But that didn't give anything either; I saw very quickly that there wasn't anything there.

What was really required was core power, core energy, core facility and functionality and to let everything come to play within myself. Otherwise, I could spend the rest of my life sitting around and talking with intellectual friends or whatever it might be, but none of this was real relationship. It fell flat for me; it really had no authenticity. It didn't really have what was required for society to function in the way that it was capable of.

By the power of open intelligence I became able to take a leap—to really make a 100% commitment, no matter what anyone else was doing or where anyone else was going—completely willing to go to any lengths to commit one's entire life to open intelligence, beyond mistake. That is a 100% priority without any other priority anywhere in sight.

THE GREATEST NATURAL RESOURCE

By the power of open intelligence we become willing, for the first time really, to see ourselves totally clearly. Through the relationship with the trainer and community we become really open to ourselves and others for the first time. We become open to ourselves the way we actually are—not our pretend fantasies and notions about what we are or what we might be. We become open to our real self, moment to moment, exactly as we are. Up and down, in one emotion or another, with one thought or another, having one sensation or another, with this, that and the other thing—extracting the power from all of it. Just letting it be real, letting it flow on by, and all the while extracting the power from it.

Our greatest natural resource is sitting right here in our own chair. All the ideas we have about what a human being is or what we're supposed to be completely fall apart. We're confronted with the reality of who we are moment to moment, and there will be a lot in that which we have probably tried to avoid, or maybe we've indulged these things impulsively without being able to control ourselves. There may be other areas of ourselves that we've tried to replace with better parts, like going to the auto mechanic and getting new brakes.

When all of this comes to a complete stop, we just stop trying to fix the flow of ordinary experience. We get totally real for the first time, letting everything be *as it is*. One day we think we're the best thing on earth, the next minute we think we are awful, and then we have all kinds of other feelings in between. We extract the power—the natural resources from within ourselves—

mining the gold from within every single datum—not getting lost in the labels, not getting lost in made-up notions about what a human being is or what a relationship is, but finding the core of ourselves that will take us through thick and thin. We find what we can really rely on no matter what.

THE POWER OF OPEN INTELLIGENCE

Open intelligence enables you, me and everyone to be able to face everything squarely, without any pretend notions or fantasies about the way things are. It means really calling the shots. If you get comfortable with your own self, then you can be comfortable in any situation; that's just the way it is. It's impossible to have any kind of relationship without having a relationship with yourself.

By the power of moment to moment open intelligence, everything just is *as it is*. Seeing that within yourself, wow, it's clear that everyone else is in exactly the same boat, and there isn't anyone in a different boat. It doesn't matter how many piles of money they have or if they have none at all, how old they are, how young they are, what kind of an education they have, what kind of education they don't have—everyone is in the same boat.

Open intelligence is greatly equalizing in a real way. It doesn't matter what anyone looks like; they can look great or they can look horrible, it really doesn't matter—open intelligence is the core. Open intelligence is the real beauty; it's the beauty of the individual, and it's the beauty and power of society. Make no mistake about that: there is no other way to cook up any kind of power or special plan or anything else; it's absolutely impossible. Either we all do it together, or we don't do it at all. It's as simple as that.

Open intelligence is exceedingly powerful. From the moment of introduction to open intelligence, it's absolutely clear that it is exceedingly powerful. From that moment on, even if there might be all kinds of data that come up, there's never any delusion about that again. It's clear from the moment of introduction that open intelligence is where it's at. There isn't anything that is anywhere else other than in open intelligence.

EXTRACT THE POWER

It takes this kind of real, decisive, direct experience of instinctive open intelligence in the moment, where every single cell of your body is drenched with aliveness. It is not some kind of spaced out or disempowered state; there is total raw, vital open intelligence that gets things done in a real way. There is no need to sit around and talk for hours about everything; you are too busy getting it done! We could all sit around and make criticisms of this, that and the other thing, but getting in there and actually changing things is much different.

Open intelligence gives us this power. We get out of the whole trip of looking to a future that is going to be so great. We also give up trying to forget about that bad past, and we get into the liveliness and vitality of what's here right now. Each one of us is totally, fully alive, vital, turned on, juiced up, ready to go, in the moment. This is what life is all about; it's about getting down and getting real.

Whatever is going on with you, it's never any more real than what is happening in this very moment. Whatever is going on with you—whether you're high, low or in between—extract the power of open intelligence. It isn't found anywhere else. Power does not require a lot of different variables in order to put it into swing. It's in whatever you're thinking—whether you're anxious, afraid, happy, ecstatic, feeling empowered or disempowered. This keeps it very simple and real.

If there are certain ways in which you seem to get blindsided, then your friends in the community will shore you up. There's no competition; everyone is in together. This is real relationship: allowing everyone to completely thrive without any hideouts, with no opportunities to dodge this way or that way or hide out in some kind of pretentious notion about who one is. It is about getting very real in the guts of everyday life, moment-to-moment, interacting with each other, living together, working together smoothly and effortlessly flowing along.

How do we find out how to do that? We do it! We show ourselves that it's real. There isn't some future to get to, some great
plan to enact. It's right now, right here, very vital, very real—
extracting the power from every single moment, just *as it is*. It
really doesn't matter what you think or what you feel; just stay
put in open intelligence, and you'll know everything you need
to know.

If there's any kind of support you need, it's always available
from clear people. Now, if you get into some kind of pickle
where you find yourself confused and lost, who are you going to
rely on—someone else who is confused and lost or someone
who's clear? Well, that's a pretty simple set of logical prin-
ciples, isn't it? It's good to know where to go for advice. If you
don't know where to go for advice, then you can't get good advice.

THE CORE POWER

There are a lot of times I meet people and they really feel limited by their circumstances, whether it is their intellectual,
emotional, or outer circumstances. On the other hand they may
feel totally expanded and out of control, as though they were the
coolest thing on earth. But open intelligence brings everything
into perspective. It allows everyone to rest in the core power
and facility of everything exactly *as it is* without any mistake
whatsoever.

By relying on that, you find out that all the labels you've applied to yourself are mistaken, including the current labels.
Whatever the label spells out, its real definition is open intelligence, and that can never be gotten away from. It's impossible
to get away from open intelligence. We learn a lot of things
about ourselves, and most of those things are mistaken. Even if
you might feel that you've gotten away from open intelligence,
it will never happen. I know for sure I've never gotten away
from open intelligence, and thus I know you won't either.

By the power of open intelligence we get to see who we really are, and it's always opening up more and more. It doesn't go
in reverse; we're always learning more about who we are.

We're always feeling more empowered, no matter what our situation, even if we're really sick or dying. When we get sick and die, the thoughts come, "Oh dear, this is so miserable and horrible. Dying is going to be a bummer and no one will want to be around me," or other thoughts like this. Or it could be crazy notions like, "I'll be able to avoid death."

By the power of open intelligence we're able to flow along with everything. It doesn't matter what it is, we know that we're going to be okay, whether it's life or death or any other datum that comes along. Some of us are old, some are young and some are in between, but it doesn't matter. Whatever the age, it is all completely fueled by open intelligence. Everything rests unavoidably in open intelligence. It's inextricably bound, which means that nothing can ever be removed from open intelligence. It's absolutely impossible. There's no delusive concept or principle you can come up with that's ever going to destroy open intelligence or take you out of the indestructible family of open intelligence.

We have all kinds of relationships in our lives, and maybe we're always looking for that special relationship; however, the truly special relationship is in the indestructible family of open intelligence. Open intelligence is indestructible. It provides an indestructible relationality that can never be destroyed, no matter what comes along—life, death or anything else. We're human beings, so we think things are a certain way, but guess what? There are many kinds of beings, not just human beings. By the power of open intelligence we're prepared for anything that happens. It doesn't have to look a certain way, and we get tuned to that through our own experience, whatever that is—one moment up, one minute down, another moment in between, all over the place. Pretty soon we start to feel consistent power all the time. We can go into any situation and we feel just fine.

NO ONE IS A STRANGER

I travel all over the world, and wherever I go I never see a stranger anywhere. I feel just as comfortable in the train station or on the airplane as I do with any of you. If I see someone crying, I want to give them a little pat or a hug. It doesn't matter whether I've ever seen them before or not—no one is a stranger. There's a total openness and connectivity. How is this provided? It's provided by open intelligence—the basic state of everything. It's natural; it's the way things are. We're naturally meant to feel connected and relational, but that doesn't mean that we always respond in one way. It could be that one time we might look very nice and be present in a loving, tender way, and in another moment it might require us to be totally fierce, ferocious and wrathful, pushing everything aside for the way of open intelligence.

By the power of open intelligence we're able to do what we've never been able to do before. It provides us a clarity-intelligence to which we would have no access without open intelligence. We have no access to real, prosperous, generous open intelligence as long as we're fumbling around in intellectualized or emotionalized definitions of what it means to be a human being.

We all have equal access to that education of open intelligence. Every single person has equal access to this beneficial open intelligence. There isn't anyone left out. It doesn't matter what kind of circumstances you have; everyone has equal access to the power of open intelligence and its very powerful benefits. The only way to extract that power is in this moment, in what you're thinking right now, in whatever emotion you're wracked with right now. Whatever it is, that's where the power of open intelligence is.

We're really getting to know ourselves in a new way. We don't have to pretend anymore; we can just relax—no more pretending. That's when life gets fun and reliable. When we know we can rely on our own open intelligence, life becomes reliable. We know that no matter what we're faced with, we're going to be able to handle it. We know too that there'll be a lot of other people right there with us. This is very important; it's very key.

A QUANTUM LEAP

It's a big, big step for humankind, and you're part of taking that quantum leap out of an intelligence that is belabored by dictionary definitions into an expansive connectivity and relationship with the entire universe. Whatever it is you're thinking or feeling right now, that is your relationship with the entire universe, right there. It's all occurring within you.

By relying on open intelligence, you really start to see how things fit together. You don't need any kind of prefabricated education to tell you about the way things are, because you're able to see it clearly and distinctly for yourself for the first time. This equal access is very important. Everyone has equal access; no one is left out. Young or old, rich or poor, beautiful or ugly, crazy or sane, it doesn't matter. All of us have equal access. When we draw on the power of this moment, it lets us see how to move in a fluid way. We don't have to have a fixed plan. We can sketch out a basic plan and then grow powerfully into it. That's the good way, that's the powerful way, that's the unerring way.

The notion of planning your life is changing. The whole way that we interpret identity, interact with identity and interact with other identities is changing right now, in this moment. In the past we were limited to one identity. Today we can have as many identities as we want to. We can go online and we can have a different identity for every single datum. We can spend hours online, a lifetime even, burrowing into the data and finding other people who will listen to it. We can have all kinds of relationships based on our data streams. By the power of open intelligence we could have dozens of beneficial, powerful identities online.

In that case the whole scheme of the Internet would be a great expression of the generosity of human beings. We want to get out there, we want to be totally open, and the Internet is evidence of that. The Internet gives us the freedom to speak out about all the things we've been holding onto. Maybe we don't want to say this or that because we might lose some friends, but on the Internet we can be ourselves and we can let it all hang out. Now, that could be negative, but it's just as likely to be positive. In fact it's more likely to be positive, because it's about people being real, talking about what's really going on as a great clarification of what it's like to be a human being. It is a great clarification of what it's like to be human, but not an end in itself. It's an eruption of generosity, an eruption of tremendous power.

As we go on with this, what we'll see is all these spews of data all over the Internet—one saying this, one saying that, one saying the other thing—are all going to settle into a pervasive quality, a pervasive power, a pervasive connectivity, a pervasive excellence, and it's all coming right out of everything being spewed out right now. Whatever the datum is, it is a display of power and generosity, of juice, of real fire, of real commitment to be who we are, with nothing holding us back.

EVERY SINGLE MOMENT IS POWERFUL

We are all built of excellence and open intelligence; no one can give that to us or take it away from us. All we have to do is show up for the relationship with open intelligence exactly as we are—high or low, up or down, this way or that. Acknowledging the basis, that's it. With that acknowledgement, every single moment is more and more powerful, and there is never an end to the stream of prosperity and generosity. Every single moment is more enlivened, more filled with the liveliness and power of open intelligence. There is no going backward; every moment there is the feeling that it can't get any better than this—but then it always does get better! That is the life that open intelligence presents to us.

Open intelligence is penetrating; it is very personal and very relational. Open intelligence is very vivid and lucid. It knows how to evaluate logically the arguments that are used to explain experience. For instance, "I can't be too committed to open intelligence. I might run out of money," or "I was committed to open intelligence, but now I am committed to money." By just sticking with open intelligence we find the thorough cut from all data, including the ideas that money has some kind of power and force of its own. Open intelligence rules over all data, including the data about money.

Open intelligence empowers generosity within the datum of money and allows for more money for more people all of the time. The strategies to save money, to hoard it and to put it somewhere have been going on our entire lives—the great plans to keep the money and to get some more of it. Open intelligence is sovereign over all data, no matter what it is. By relying on our own open intelligence we allow an expanse of generosity to naturally open up.

If we collapse into any datum, then everything starts to look like it. If we collapse into the money datum, then everything looks like the money datum. If we collapse into our fixed political frameworks—whether they are progressive or conservative or whatever they are—everything kind of looks like that. We are looking at everything from that vantage, but that's a very narrow tunnel, which just keeps going on and on always with more data related to that initial datum—money, progressive politics, conservative politics or whatever it is.

SUPER-INTELLIGENCE

By relying on open intelligence, a vivid and lucid intelligence opens up. It becomes possible to see that we really are fueled by a very connecting intelligence, one that takes care of everything, one where we know we really are capable and can get things done. It is an intelligence through which we can be prosperous and generous with each other, sharing openly an abundance of all kinds of resources we never even dreamt of until we started extracting the power of open intelligence.

I see this as absolutely true in my own experience, and I know it to be the case. If any datum seems to jump up and grab you in one way or another, rely on open intelligence. Open intelligence will prevail with its vivid understanding and lucid intellect in the midst of all experience. We have within us a power and capability that is really unparalleled, and we show that to ourselves in open intelligence. It won't come from anywhere else.

The real core importance is open intelligence—shining forth from within all experience, the spontaneous release of all experience, the un-capturability of the here-and-now. There isn't any way to really make anything out of the here-and-now, to capture it or define it or fix it in any way. Even the idea that we can have any fixed attitudes or data sets about ourselves—it's really totally impossible. The moment we think that we have a fixed idea of ourselves, where is it? It's impossible to capture it anywhere.

So, the commitment to open intelligence is really key. The more we hear about data, the more it seems to be the way things are. With all those definitions in the dictionary, it seems exactly like that: each definition seems to have an independent nature. We convince ourselves, we really do. However, we're completely at choice in every single moment as to how we see the world, how we see our perceptions. We're completely at choice, 100% at choice.

The here-and-now is a revelation of our own choice; it isn't anything other than that. The need to be okay with ourselves is as simple as just relaxing and letting everything be *as it is*, whether we're being hard on ourselves or exalting ourselves. I know in my own experience that what is required is the total commitment to the authenticity of open intelligence.

The introduction to open intelligence is so rich, so authentic and so real that it's impossible to escape it or to create any other kind of reality or any other kind of definition of the way things are. There really isn't any need to come to any conclusion about any definition about anything, because the moment there's a definition about a particular relationship or love or anything like that, in the next moment it's undone, whatever was thought about the moment before. Again and again there's the self-release of what is here and now and an impossibility of holding on to that. Just by the power of hearing that message repeatedly, it becomes obvious, in the same way that data had become obvious as a reality.

COMPLETE FREEDOM

A baby has no idea about the independent nature of anything. There is no connection to the datum "me," no ideas about any of that. The supposed independent nature of everything is all learned, and everyone is always completely able to choose their perception about that. No one is ever a victim of what they've learned, not ever. No one is held to any perception that occurred before this moment; it's impossible.

The identity is really an accumulation of definitions and past data. It's an accumulation of all our thoughts, all our emotions, all our sensations, all our other experiences up to that point. We just assume this is our identity, because that's what we've learned. However, upon the introduction to open intelligence, that identity doesn't seem so fixed and real any longer, because open intelligence is totally convincing, right here. There isn't a need to haul in an entire vocabulary of past experience in order to identify oneself. "Oh, who am I? Well, somebody stepped on my toe when I was two and I hit him in the face, and I've been a bully ever since." I think you get where I'm going with that!

This process becomes very ingrained: accumulating all the data and saying "yes" to it. "All this data that I've had all these years, that's who I am. Here I am, all this data, and I have a lot of paperwork to back it up: my résumé, CV, diplomas, birth certificate. Here's my proof; this is who I am." That's one way of looking at it; however, it doesn't provide any sustenance. That's a mere appraisal of events, but no accumulation of data is any kind of conclusive evidence of who we are.

The very moment of open intelligence is the only conclusive evidence ever of who we are. In that there is complete freedom from all fixed frameworks whatsoever. Not just freedom, but also absolute courage—total absolute courage, simple and complete in itself with no point of reference as to accumulated identity and no points of reference into the future about any destination where one is heading. To enter into a relationship with oneself on that basis is to be like an infant—to be that open and that vulnerable to whatever is presenting itself in the moment.

It can seem a little jarring or disconcerting if we have had a lot of fixed ideas about ourselves, and then all of a sudden open intelligence is alive and real. Here we had all these ideas; we knew exactly who we were, and now all of a sudden it doesn't look that way at all, and so it can feel like the bottom has fallen out. Whatever seemed to be supporting that identity isn't there anymore. At the same time, everything we've accomplished up to that point starts to make a lot of sense.

There's no need whatsoever to have any kind of notion about what open intelligence is, and the same is true in regard to relationship. When I was young I had all kinds of ideas about marriage and having children, along with ideas about religion, psychiatry, psychology, philosophy, mathematics, science, computers and so on, but they have absolutely no relevance whatsoever—other than as totally open intelligence. Open intelligence subsumes all these built-up accumulations of data that we have about ourselves and the accumulation of identity. It's completely undone in the super-factual reality of the here-and-now. It's like pressing a reset button in every single moment. Everything is reset to the core in every single moment. In that is true piercing intelligence that knows what to do and how to act.

PRESSING THE RESET BUTTON

There are countless people who are totally interested and committed to open intelligence, so there's instantaneous community and relationship everywhere. If you want to make it your priority to partner up with people who are committed to open intelligence, you have a perfect right to do so, or if you don't want to do that, you have a perfect right to do that as well. It's all entirely up to you.

Many times we learn a lot of things from our cultures that limit our choices, and some of those things might be very ingrained in us. For instance, if we grow up in a culture where there is royalty, then in that culture there are the royal persons and the lesser royal persons and the absolutely un-royal persons. Maybe we thought, "Oh well, I'm doomed. By an accident of birth I'm not a royal," or, "I have the wrong karma," or, "I wasn't born in the Garden of Eden," or whatever it might be. We may not even recognize these data unless we boil everything down to its essence and clearly see them.

All data shine within the view of open intelligence; the view shines from within all its points of view. This creates a great equalness within us, and we can see how we've adopted all this data in a way that may have been damaging in some way and which may have lessened our assurance and our security within ourselves. These ideas that I'm talking about can be great sources of oppression. By relying on open intelligence, all of the ideas that we've used to oppress ourselves, to dampen our assurance and innate confidence are all set free. It doesn't mean we need to change them; it means we get to really see them.

By relying on open intelligence all the data are illuminated so that we see that data have no hold and that they have no way to keep anything in place. Data do not have an independent nature and have no force or reality of their own. Just the simplicity of that is the very greatest strength anyone will ever have. There's no need to expect anything other than that out of life, because that is where everything comes from. That is the source of the power of enactment and the power of liveliness in every moment.

Many times when we hear about open intelligence we think, "At last, an escape from all data streams. I want to get out of data and get into open intelligence. I don't want to be a self, I don't want to be an "I," I don't want to be a mind, so now I'm going to be this other thing." Well, light your finger on fire and tell me that you have no self! There is no separate intelligence outside of you and me. That's where the rubber hits the road. There's nothing to be done with data, and there's no escape from "you." That's real freedom.

The process of the Empowerments really helps us see how everything that we've gone through in our life is illuminated by open intelligence. It doesn't matter what we've thought about our past or what we've done in our past; it is of no consequence whatsoever in this moment. Everything is completely resolved and released right here. That's all we can rely on.

All the expectations for the future—the right relationship, the right job, the right amount of money—will never be anything other than the ever clear here-and-now. It is ever clear, so there isn't any destination to get to or any accumulated identity to get rid of or change. It's right here and right now. By the consequence of your own direct experience of open intelligence, you are convinced—no other way.

Listening to a lot of talks on open intelligence is like pressing the reset button again and again. After a lifetime of hearing, reading and writing every other thing about yourself and who you are, now it's the reset button, hearing it again and again—reset, reset, reset: "Oh yeah, that's right; oh yeah, that's right." The resonance grows strong, reverberating throughout everything without doubt, without confusion. Confusion disappears forever. In confusion itself there is freedom from confusion, and that is the end of confusion. In the datum of confusion there is the spontaneous illumination of open intelligence—the end of confusion.

With doubt it is the same way: in doubt itself there is the self-arising bliss of no doubt, which is not a separate state from doubt itself. Freedom from confusion *in* confusion, not separate from confusion; the inseparability of everything from your own shining open intelligence. This makes talks on identity very simple!

Value Letters from Participants

My first experiences of Balanced View three years ago resulted in the single biggest shift that has ever occurred in my life. The first few open meetings and teachings showed me that the potential of humans that I had dreamt of was not only possible but already a reality, as demonstrated by the founder and the committed community of this recently-born Balanced View organization.

Many very simple interactions with people who were relying on open intelligence brought about significant shifts within me. For example, before I had been to a Balanced View meeting I was walking past a person on the street who looked at me with such openness and greeted me in a most profound, deeply caring way that I was shocked. I had hardly felt such love from another human being before, let alone from a complete stranger. Upon attending my first open meeting, I saw that this person was present and was one of the Balanced View trainers.

What I had dreamt possible as the potential of human society was being demonstrated by normal people in everyday life in an uncontrived way. To be able to suddenly experience this in my own life was like winning the lottery, but of incomparably greater value.

The first time I saw Candice in a public setting, she walked into a room of roughly 80 people who were waiting to hear her talk, some of whom were only there to criticize and debate with her, and I was simply amazed by what I saw. Candice entered the room completely worry-free—to the extent that you could actually feel her peace. There was no rush, no anxiety, no defending, nothing. She simply stood in front of the audience smiling for a while, like someone who was seeing a dear and close friend for the first time in many years. Before taking her seat and without any vocal communication she had already pre-empted all debate and responded to all doubts.

I could recognize that the full power in all human beings had blossomed in this person who sat in front of me and who was demonstrating countless fruits of benefit, including the ability to answer questions in a way that left me filled with clarity and insight. What I would eventually find over time was a capacity in her to facilitate, guide and nurture a community of human beings towards their own blossoming and the full-on willingness and readiness to deal with unwavering orientation towards the benefit of all with all of the dynamic and unpredictable situations that will inevitably arise in such a role.

Here was a teaching and a teacher that didn't hold back in any way, which communicated frankly and directly, and which was available to anyone who had an open mind. This accord of open and willing people with an immensely clear and powerful teaching brought about transformation all around me—and within me as well. The results were so powerful. I honored and loved not only the teaching but also the openness and courage of my fellow participants. The very same words apply now to this retreat.

SECOND SHARE

Thank you for being here with all of us in this most meaningful way. There are many forms of service to people; however, to identify the most essential of all forms of service—which is to lead people to total reliance on open intelligence and then to commit to providing this in the most deeply considered and effective way—is incomparable in its value.

The fact that you did this, un-awed by inevitable difficulties and challenges, astounds and inspires me. If you had compromised your vision in any way for the sake of some convenience or temporary end, my life would have remained a sorry contrivance. However, as an outcome of the direct decisions you made, my life has had the necessary supportive factors to be completely transformed into one of self-present fearlessness and abundance. And to think I am only one example of so many!

I see the benefits of the Four Mainstays in my dearest friends from the community here at the Center and other Balanced View communities that I have had the honor to visit. They are so powerful, so able to inspire others, so able to get people working together as a team. By the power of their joy, people simply want to help. They are experts of self-leadership and team leadership, and they foster the same expertise in everyone they meet, constantly and lovingly fanning the flames of the strengths, gifts and talents in people. The most incredibly developed structure of conventional leadership could never create this magic that happens when people are simply happy as they are. The Four Mainstays are the field from which communities like this naturally sprout.

THIRD SHARE

I found some of my old journals the other day, and I had been writing for years about how I longed for open intelligence and a balanced view and about how my negative states were hindering my desire for perfection. What a relief to find this training! I had thought that I needed to not have negative thoughts, emotions or sensations in order to have open intelligence. I thought perfection would be achieved through a lot of effort and through purification of negativity, but my hopes were always dashed.

Open, fierce connectivity with my trainers in my everyday activities propelled me into a loving, respectful, honest, caring relationship with myself, my trainer and everyone else. Open intelligence and perfection was the only training I've received. I realized the value in being completely open to my trainer, hiding nothing and going to any lengths to correct inappropriate activities. By this I mean that I realized I had to step-up my commitment to stop indulging, avoiding and replacing my life circumstances. I sometimes felt total humiliation and fear, yet I remained steadfast in my commitment and easily could see the data of being a victim playing out. I realized there was nowhere to run and hide.

My trainer's totally loving, direct and wrathful guidance has infused in me such confidence, gratitude and respect that I feel forever grateful for what I've received. I'm continually learning and refining my body, speech, mind, qualities and activities. I do so with the constant reminder to be gentle on myself. Making it into a project is just falling back into the victim viewpoint. The results are deepening insights into everything, more energy, more flexibility and deeper caring and compassion. Attitudes of gratitude and respect replace negative behavior, and generosity and compassion shine forth.

It just feels so good to hear and read the trainings; it's like the roar of a lion and the loving care of a mother's warm embrace at the same time. It's the coolest thing I could hear and never sounds corny. The daily results are just endless, so much so that I have to look for disturbances and painful data and I think, "Do they even exist?"

The fears of losing out, of being held hostage or of being rejected are just lousy memories, fading away like a burnt out light bulb. Grey, tight faces are warmed till exploding with natural radiance. People feel totally empowered in an authentic way—not some kind of blissed-out, weird, culty, disempowered, numb kind of way. It's awesome to witness people awaken to their true power to be of utmost benefit to everyone. Wow! Thank you so much Candice for this precious time together. In love, respect, gratitude and service.

Day Two

EMPOWERING HUMAN SOCIETY

The Written Text and Commentary

(The written text is in bold)
(The commentary is in normal script)

The process of indestructible open intelligence identity is summed up in education and empowerment of society, individually and collectively. Education refers to the process of educating oneself and all of society in open intelligence—the very powerful balanced view. This takes place through the Four Mainstays of Balanced View. The first Mainstay is the simple practice of short moments of open intelligence. This is the key button to press for everyone—the reset button for human society.

The second is the written instructions, which radically increase the momentum and power of open intelligence. Have you noticed that? Open intelligence—it's on and you feel fantastic, and then you hear a certain instruction and, wow, open intelligence is even more expansive and spacious and powerful than you already were convinced that it was. There's nowhere to go. There's no destination, nothing to get to. These instructions are very pivotal, very key.

Again, everyone receives exactly the instructions needed to empower the beneficial, prosperous, generous qualities and activities of open intelligence. Every single person in this room has taken part in the written instruction by participating in the Empowerments. So, there's a standardized training that everyone can participate in and for the whole world to come to understand ourselves as we really are.

Then in addition to that there is the support of the trainers and the community. Every single one of us needs not only the standardized instruction, we need the personal connection. There will be times that come up where someone with more experience in open intelligence, so to speak, will be able to support us greatly. They'll be able to share a key point that completely unravels our whole way of being with a certain set of data. Not only the standardized instruction is important, but this personal connection as well.

It doesn't matter if we're here in this organization or in another organization. If we want to lead in a powerful way, we need to obtain the consent of everyone on that team to commit to open intelligence; otherwise, that team cannot be empowered. If one person on the team is relying on open intelligence, it'll be empowered a little bit, but it's nothing like having everyone buy in. When the team buys into open intelligence, it creates a momentum way beyond that of the individual. The standardized instructions are important, but also this custom connection is really important too.

There'll always be certain data streams in *everyone* to which that one is completely blind. This custom connection with an empowered trainer and community allows clear seeing to open up in a safe, comfortable environment where one can encounter all one's data and extract the power from them.

It doesn't matter where we are or what we're up to. Say, we're an environmentalist. That's an area of work that is just totally beautiful and powerful and one in which many wonderful changes have been created. We need even greater power in the area of environmentalism or in any area of human knowledge. The way to really ramp up that power is to have a team working on that problem or issue, whatever it is, with the whole team committed to open intelligence.

We work with teams all over the world like this who are committed to open intelligence. And how do we do that? We have the power of our own example. We've done it here. We've created a worldwide organization through open intelligence-teaming. That's why that map looks the way it does. *(Note: The participants had been shown a map of all the places in the world where people had logged in to the Great Free-dom/Balanced View web site.)* It's due to everyone in the team making the commitment to open intelligence.

The trainers are people who support each individual in optimizing the instructions for powerful, everyday open intelligence. Maybe when you're introduced to open intelligence the afflictive states are just too much, and you just don't know how open intelligence is going to possibly be continuous in afflictive states. Maybe you've been like that—I know I have been in the past—but what I found is that open intelligence is the only solution. Open intelligence is extracted from the afflictive states.

I found that personally to be a lot of fun. Wow. I can just let it all flow on by. Powerful at the core. There's nothing to do about all the labels. Brilliantly shining from within those labels is an incredible power that I had never learned about and an intelligence I never knew I had. Open intelligence is self-affirming. It says "No, you don't need to go that way. You don't need to go with all the data which supposedly describe everything about who you are. You don't need to relate to people that way. You can live a life *completely* different from anyone else on earth if you want to and be perfectly fine."

By the power of open intelligence we really unite ourselves, and compassion naturally rises up, but not as some kind of thing we have to practice or cultivate. It's the wrathful compassion of seeing ourselves as we actually are. So the trainer can help us with that. They might point out things that we had no idea about. With all of us we have certain ways of operating that can be cleared up instantaneously. I'm thinking of an example of a woman who was very competitive with other women—competing for the attention of men or financial security—but she had no idea that she had this data set. A trainer with experience in human living and in confronting afflictive states can be greatly helpful by pointing things out that we never knew had taken control of us. This was just an example.

It doesn't mean it applies to everyone here, but it does apply to many people, even though we may not even realize that we may have been subtly competing with others for financial security or for attention. A relationship based on open intelligence really opens your eyes. We get to see ourselves as we really are, and we get to take responsibility for ourselves as we are.

Using the example I mentioned before, if we're competing with others for money or some kind of attention, where we need attention, understanding or security from others, then we're always going to be limited by data. If we get really jealous and we can't stand it if our partner looks at somebody else or if they spend time with someone else, what is the solution? To control our partner's behavior? To control our own behavior?

Rather than trying to control anything, we let everything be *as it is*. We can see just how jealous we all are, and through that recognition the jealousy is normalized. We come to terms with it within ourselves and we mine the power from it. We find that in jealousy there's actually a powerful force. It's a powerful force of being able to accomplish whatever we set out to do. That's the power that is naturally extracted from out of control jealousy. All these thoughts and feelings that may be withheld from oneself can be normalized by letting them be as they are.

Relying on open intelligence doesn't mean sitting in all the data, getting into them or acting them out in some kind of berserk way. It means relying on open intelligence, relying on the Four Mainstays for everything to be *as it is*, supporting each other when difficult patches come up. "I'm right here. I'll sit here with you, and we'll just be together." All those red dots on the worldwide map—they represent the togetherness, the whole field of understanding of exactly what it is you're going through.

These afflictive states are very powerful. Many people say, "Oh, I'm not jealous," but pretty soon they find out they're jealous to the core—it had just been hidden. All of these thoughts, emotions, sensations and ways of labeling things are within the normal range of human experience, and we get to normalize them for the first time, and we get to see how data have controlled our relationship to ourself and our relationship with others. This isn't rocket science; at the same time it's very bold and courageous.

Because open intelligence isn't a special state, there is no way it can be faked. It is present equally in everything, pervading everything evenly and equally, and everything opens up in a natural way. Everything is spacious, vast, powerful, lively and filled with a lot of power and juice. There is no time frame whatsoever; open intelligence didn't begin anytime and it won't end anytime. That's what "no time frame" means.

Open intelligence is indestructible. No matter what happens to you, it is impossible to get out of open intelligence. If you were destroyed, nothing would happen to open intelligence. If a meteor hit the planet Earth and—*boom*—the whole thing was blown up, nothing would happen to open intelligence. This is the indestructible basis, the indestructible basis of all data, the powerful view of open intelligence. If the whole planet Earth could explode but nothing would happen to open intelligence, what does that say about our afflictive states?

It's impossible to package data in a way that will bring comfort and power. There would always be more wanting and more unmanageability. The very nature of trying to package identity into a data set *is* unmanageability, powerlessness and helplessness. That is the very nature of trying to package human identity into data. We're much more powerful than the limiting identifications we have taken on in our lives. When we get to know ourselves as we are, we relax. We relax completely, and at the same time we have way more power. We're able to do things we never dreamt of or imagined before.

The trainers are an amazing support in these afflictive states, because we might suffer for the rest of our life if we never let someone know us well enough to point something out. The safety of a relationship with a trainer based on open intelligence is a tremendous refuge. It is a totally tremendous refuge of complete and total safety, and in that relationship there's enough relaxation to let everything be *as it is*. We know we're okay no matter what comes up.

The trainer is someone who has the presence of continuous open intelligence. They've been willing to enter into all their own afflictive states. That's the only reason any trainer can support anyone else. It hasn't been through getting into some kind of high special state that's different from everybody else and then protecting that and pointing out to them how they're wrong. It's by the deep dive into the afflictive states—all the ones that we've wanted to avoid: greed, anger, pride, lust, envy, gluttony, sloth—and letting them be as they are.

This isn't really what we've learned at all. We've learned that we're going to be okay if we package all our data into a certain identity package, but we find that our power and success really isn't in that at all. It's in the deep dive: extracting the power from the afflictive states.

The fourth Mainstay is the worldwide Balanced View community on all continents, in all local communities and online, Balanced View cultivates powerful community. Within clarity community we see how it works for everyone to rely on the Four Mainstays to create potent solutions for change, individual and collective—this is the actual empowerment of society from the grassroots. Everything that you see right here at the Balanced View Center and that is represented by those dots all over the world is due to the potency of connecting with others in that way that brings it all about. It comes from the grassroots, and the best education we can possibly get is right here within ourselves. If we don't have this education in open intelligence, we'll be unable to truly take advantage of any other education we have.

Rather than focusing on data, we suggest solutions that we ourselves can implement. That's how this whole movement came about. People don't sit around and criticize and complain. Everyone contributes whatever solution they can to making the whole team work. Everything flows together seamlessly, and it all works in a very powerful way. It's not wimpy.

We suggest solutions and then we implement them. There is no need to suggest a solution without being able to implement it. If you have a solution, then think through what's needed to implement it, and then talk to someone else. That's the time to present a solution and get it into action.

For example, if we want a center in our local area like this beautiful Center here, we build it ourselves with the support of other people who will help us. That's how this Center in Sweden came about: people connecting together to make this place happen, and this is the same way with open intelligence community. Beauty and harmony arise out of a way of being together that is completely comfortable and at the same time totally powerful—totally enacting change that really works within ourselves and collectively.

We take complete responsibly for development of a strong healthy local community by emphasizing the importance of the Four Mainstays. The strength of our local community depends on the Four Mainstays. This is a simple structure that really works to unite people all over the world. At the local community level each individual has complete responsibility for maintaining the vitality of the community by relying on the Four Mainstays. If everyone's relying on the Four Mainstays, there's no data stream that can take over. There is no one who can arise to bully everybody else in the group, no extra loud voices that get to talk about everything while no one else gets to say anything. Unified, harmonious, flowing community arises by the power of the Four Mainstays, where everyone can contribute their strengths, gifts and talents.

This is very important. It is an absolute key. The Four Mainstays create an indestructible culture of gratitude and respect which is quite distinct from the way society usually operates. We had a lot of notions about how society could be, and we were right! We actually see it in action: we are living harmoniously, peacefully and powerfully together, and that is really convincing. It all comes from right here within ourselves.

First we allow the community of our data to be in harmony. It flows along effortlessly in a culture of gratitude and respect. That is the culture of open intelligence: one of gratitude and respect within ourselves. We're not trying to turn anything on or off. Everything is allowed to be *as it is*. From this community of data at rest within ourselves, we're able to really extend our-

31

selves to others in a beautiful way and to contribute our strengths, gifts and talents in a very powerful way.

Thus, when we enter into the indestructible open intelligence-community, the commitment to the power of community is found in these Four Mainstays. We utilize the Four Mainstays to get into action exhibiting the power of open intelligence to create revolutionary change in human society. Each community throughout the world elects a group delegate who represents their activities at our annual world conference. Every year we have a world conference and people come together representing the concerns of their community. In this way everyone is allowed a voice. We have an actual process for allowing the voice of every single person to be heard and to have that enter into the way that the whole organization actually unfolds. This is the meaning of a grassroots organization. It comes up from community—from the heart of human society itself into reality.

It is built from the grassroots of human society by individuals like you and me who together show the world the powerful, new human identity—indestructible open intelligence. These are the Four Mainstays: open intelligence, training, the trainer and the community, and together they form the indestructible vehicle of open intelligence. In open intelligence is the perfect family—the indestructible open intelligence-family. No bad events are going to happen in the open intelligence-family. Open intelligence maintains and sustains everything, no matter its label.

The Four Mainstays are like four legs of a chair. The chair must have all four legs; otherwise, it is of no use. If a chair has less than four legs, it will take a great deal of energy to sit in it, and it will be of no real support. It will be more effort than it is worth to try to sit in the chair. However, when the chair has all four legs, we can rely on it without any effort, without anything needing to be done. The chair is available and we can count on it.

32

Likewise, in the practice of open intelligence, all Four Mainstays are required for radical empowerment of the individual and for radical empowerment of all of society. When all Four Mainstays are present, everyone is mutually strong and empowered by open intelligence.

Even though it has taken human society millions of years to get to the point of recognition of open intelligence, this momentum will quickly take over all of society, and many of us sitting here today will live to see happy, healthy human society. It's really true.

Like each drop of rainfall produces the power of mighty rivers, lakes and oceans, each person who practices open intelligence creates a powerful, sane human culture. It is up to you and it is up to me. Together we are a powerful society. We empower society through open intelligence. We create a great, indivisible force of open intelligence.

Day Two Talk

Where people are committed to open intelligence, teamwork becomes effortless and easy. There is no interruption by any datum, and people don't get completely derailed in a lot of opinionated conversations about what's going on. The spread of Balanced View worldwide is due to open intelligence. People are able to cooperate and work together in a unified powerful fashion for change.

Wherever we are, whoever we are, we are individually responsible for adopting the Four Mainstays. The Mainstays are like the legs of a four legged chair. If a chair has one leg missing, you have to balance so that you don't fall over. With the support of the key instructions in the training, with the support of a trainer and with the support of the community, then there are four legs to the chair. There isn't all the energy that is required to balance a chair with fewer than four legs. Some people might say, "Oh well, I don't need anything. I can just practice open intelligence on my own," then they have a chair with only one leg. Just imagine trying to sit on a chair with one leg!

When people come here to the Balanced View Center, one of the things they usually mention is that it's just so comfortable to be here. This is because everyone is committed to open intelligence. We know where it's at with ourselves and with others, so we're not confused at all anymore about who we are or what our responsibility is in terms of interactions with others. It's very simple and straightforward, and this all comes about through open intelligence. When people come together, it's fun instead of being a drag.

OPEN INTELLIGENCE AS THE CORE DEFINITION

In a lot of relationships we learn that it's normal to be up and down all the time and that relationships and our inner life are supposed to be up and down. Most of us accept that fate. "Well, I guess this is just the way it is." However, upon introduction to open intelligence we find we have a solid core. In ballet a body core is developed, and in order for a ballerina to be fantastic there must be a solid core. Every single movement depends on the solid core, and the more solid the core the more powerful the performance.

The same is true with open intelligence. It is absolutely the core, and open intelligence comes about through the interaction with others in daily life. We're pack animals and we like to hang out together. Even if we go live in a cave, we will still be thinking about everybody. We're not going to be in there just thinking about ourselves; we're going to bring everybody else in there with us. Most of all we bring *ourselves*, because wherever we go, there we are, and we can't get away from that. We can never get away from our circumstantial data, whatever it is. Our circumstances have generated certain data, and we've labeled it in certain ways.

At some point we're introduced to open intelligence, and we find that it is the core definition—it's the core definition in all labels. Then we don't have to be confused anymore. It's just open intelligence and data—completely inseparable, just like space is inseparable from air. There is no confusion any longer and nothing to worry about. In relationships, sex and all these other issues, there is nothing to worry about. In open intelligence the answer will be revealed.

NORMALIZE ALL OF YOUR EXPERIENCE

Let's say that you're practicing open intelligence, but you completely forget about it and jump into bed with somebody. Then all the adventitious data will just play out with no open intelligence. The only way to continue on is to practice open intelligence in that circumstance. Whoever we are, we have our own sexual data streams. One person has this data set and another person another set, and it's just as varied as the drops of water in the ocean. Whatever the data are, the practice is the same.

A fantastic sexual experience has nothing to do with the way you're moving or what you're thinking or feeling. Really. The key is to normalize all of your experience in ever great open intelligence, to extract the power of what you think, what you feel and what you sense by practicing open intelligence. In this way open intelligence is continuous. The sexual domain is a very powerful domain for the practice of open intelligence. You get into all kinds of thoughts and emotions that you never really knew you had. "Oh, I better be doing this or I better be doing that or maybe this is right and that's wrong, and better not be thinking this."

We are sexual beings, and being sexual is normal, and when we practice open intelligence we get to see just how sexual we are. We don't hide out from it anymore. Pretty soon everybody looks attractive! We find that we've been kind of damping things down. "Oh, it might be wrong to feel sexually attracted to everyone and everything. That would just be too overwhelming." Moment-to-moment open intelligence is the perspective, just like the perspective of a flawless crystal ball pervades all of its reflections. The same is true with your own spacious open intelligence. Whatever's going on for you, it's just the way it is.

If the sexual domain is of interest to you, no partner is required. A partner is an option, but a partner is not required for sexual experience. Many of these things you can explore on your own; you have permission to do so! If it doesn't feel safe or if you don't feel you can quite practice open intelligence or if it isn't continuous during sexual experience, just have some fun with yourself. Fool around a little bit, see what gets going and normalize your thinking.

The dynamics of sexuality are totally simple, but there's no way to have any kind of great sexual experience with another human being without being able to have a great sexual experience with yourself. The basis is to normalize everything you think and feel, to just gradually become accustomed to that in an easygoing way. Many times we learn certain taboos about sexual behavior. We all have things we think are right, other things we think are wrong, things that are scary, things that we would never want to do, things we want to do but we never have. By the power of relying on the core competence of open intelligence, we get to normalize all this data.

In the sexual domain, data can be very frenetic, just like in the dream state, where it can go out of control. It's a very powerful domain of open intelligence, because we get to really see just how data flow along inseparably from open intelligence. There isn't any datum that has a special hold or which can disempower you in any way. By really understanding ourselves in this way we become responsible sexually. It isn't that everything goes pell-mell and we just run around acting on our urges. Responsibility emerges—responsibility in open intelligence.

We find that all the impulses we had that we thought meant we were in love are just impulses. We find that when sexual feelings come up, it does not mean we have to act on them, shut them down, avoid them or replace them with something else. In the sexual domain the core competence of open intelligence applies, and it is very, very powerful in that it provides complete freedom of choice. If we do not have responsibility and complete freedom of choice in our sexual experience, we cannot have it anywhere else in our life.

To not be led around any longer by sexual impulses is extremely potent. This is a great teacher and a great domain of open intelligence-activity. In open intelligence, for the first time we truly know what real love is. We can see clearly; so, if sexual feelings come up, we can see exactly how acting on those feelings would play out. We're no longer led around by the sexual feelings. We can see the effect they'd have on us and the effect they'd have on other people, and we become much less likely to act irresponsibly. At the same time we empower ourselves for optimal sexual relating that really is fun and free—the kind of sex we always wanted but never have had.

SEXUAL RESPONSIBILITY

Usually there are ideas: "Oh yeah, I want to eventually have the perfect sexual experience." Maybe we have a great sexual experience and we think, "Oh boy, now I know how to do it. Now I'm going to do this thing again and again and ensure my sexual experience." In open intelligence we find the vitality and power of sexual experience, and this frees us up a lot. Otherwise, sexual desire is a datum that is always kind of lurking around in the background.

If we confront all of our data about sexuality and get real with them—the way we *really* feel rather than the way we'd like to pretend—that's very opening and very spacious. If you're driving down the street and you see all the highway workers out there and they all look good, just let that be *as it is*. If you're having experiences like that, it's a good sign; you're opening up to the full range of experience and connection.

Sexuality is not a datum that has a special power. It's the domain of open intelligence, just like any other datum. By allowing everything to be *as it is*, we're really greatly empowered in this area, and it isn't so scary anymore. You may not feel that you are afraid of sex, but believe me, by practicing open intelligence you'll learn a lot about yourself and the sexual domain, no matter how old you get. We all are products of culture; we all learn different things. We all have our fantasies, our special thoughts, our special feelings and our special sensations. We each are whoever we are in that way and it's really important to normalize that.

Sometimes people have sexual longings that they think are completely inappropriate, and sometimes these data come up and completely take control. When these data arise, the key is open intelligence. This is the sovereign guide that will show us a way to responsible behavior. The only way we can have complete sovereignty over the data is to let them be within ourselves. There we'll learn how to act responsibly.

There are many sexual activities carried out that are irresponsible, and as a human society we've struggled with population growth. Why do we struggle with population growth, even though we have pills, condoms, special foams and fairy dust and who knows what else to try to control the population growth? Has it worked? No, because the problem isn't in the birth control methods; the problem is in us. We have to understand ourselves more, and we have to bring ourselves into the place of open intelligence. Let that open up within our sexual experience—that's the only way we will ever have population control.

If we're unable to decide what to do when a sexual impulse comes up, then we might end up in a situation we didn't want to have, but by the power of open intelligence we never have to end up in a situation we don't want to be in. Why? Because we're no longer led around by primitive impulses. Sexual feelings are perfectly normal, but if we don't know what to do with them, they become primitive impulses and drives that can lead us around in the way that a puppeteer leads a puppet around. We really don't want to live that way, individually or as a society.

By the power of open intelligence we have real solidity within ourselves, and so we don't require a relationship any longer to make us whole. We don't get into a state of needy anxiety like, "Oh man, living by myself is too much. I've got to find someone else to be with." A world of single people would be just fine! If your choice is to be on your own and not couple up, it's all fine. Whatever you decide, the key is responsibility. Open intelligence allows optimal sexual experience—coupled with responsibility—so that's really powerful. Everyone who loves sex, and that's just about everyone, really wants to be able to be responsible and clear. It's a lot of fun to increase open intelligence in this domain.

OPEN INTELLIGENCE IN DREAMS AND SLEEP

Just like with dreaming or sleep where we might feel we lose control of open intelligence—sexual feelings are very powerful domains in which to practice open intelligence. If we practice open intelligence in our sexual experience and also when we're asleep and dreaming, and we get a strong sense of open intelligence—real continuous open intelligence coming alive in those domains—then we don't feel threatened by things any longer. We have thought either subtly or overtly that there were things beyond our control, like our sexual impulses or dreaming and sleeping. "Oh, when I go to sleep I have no control whatsoever," or, "When I have those dreams, they're so scary. I'm there but I don't have any control."

While falling asleep, maintain open intelligence; it's as simple as that. You get to a place where everything sort of blanks out; it's impossible to have a thought even if you want to. That's called a thought-free state, and even though it doesn't have any thoughts, it has a name—"thought-free state"—but that's just another datum. By the power of extracting open intelligence in that thought-free state while going to sleep, open intelligence is seen as the basis of all the data associated with dreaming and sleeping, just as it is the basis for all data occurring during the daytime.

If you just check this out, you will get a sense of it, but don't try too hard, because that's not the point. Just by the practice of open intelligence, it will come alive in your dreams and sleep. Any of these real life issues such as sexuality, dreaming and sleeping are fostered so very powerfully and potently in community with other people who are practicing open intelligence. Just that connection alone is totally powerful, totally powerful in an inexpressible way.

TAKING ADVANTAGE OF THE FOUR MAINSTAYS

In building your local community of Balanced View and Great Freedom, the Four Mainstays are the core. With the Four Mainstays everyone contributes solutions; people aren't sitting around all the time talking about data. There's alive and vital contribution to the health of the community. Each person is responsible for practicing open intelligence in a simple way and for maintaining that core comfortable environment for everyone else who comes into community. In this incredible worldwide movement no one can ever be kicked out, and no one can be kept from coming in.

It's entirely up to each of us. I know what I see and what other trainers report to me, and that is that the participants who take advantage of the Four Mainstays are the ones who grow strong. This is just the way it is. Otherwise, it's kind of easy to get derailed.

Now, many of us have never been in any kind of environment where there is a culture of complete gratitude and respect that is totally spontaneous. However, by the power of open intelligence, a culture of gratitude and respect naturally develops, just like right here at the Great Freedom Centre in Sweden. A culture of gratitude and respect is totally natural and spontaneous. Due to open intelligence we understand each other deeply and we understand ourselves deeply. It's due to the laser-like piercing discernment of open intelligence.

HOW RELATIONSHIP IS MEANT TO BE

We're able to really see that no datum works as a basis for relationship and that it's open intelligence that makes everything effortlessly flow along. It's amazing that you can get up in the morning, and the day before you had been working all day long side by side with everyone else, and in the morning you can't wait to get up and do it again! This is really what relationship is supposed to be like. This is our natural state, our natural way of relating.

In open intelligence things really come alive. We can just relax; all the trying to have the right data is over. Have you ever felt in a relationship, "Oh, if I just have the right data the other person will like me"? Oh dear. But then we can never quite find the right data sets. Let's say we're a conservative politico or a progressive one, and even if we have our conservative or progressive data sets, when we get together with other people who say they have conservative or progressive data sets, their data may not be like ours at all, because they're a different kind of conservative or progressive. There's never any real coming together, no real continuity of relationship and care between people when it's all based on data.

In open intelligence we just automatically feel connected. The more we understand ourselves, the more we understand exactly how everyone else ticks. Open intelligence and data being inseparable, there's no puzzle any longer.

We don't need thick manuals or facts filling up our hard drive to try to figure out who we are. Have you ever seen any of those manuals that have all the different ways to diagnose psychological or psychiatric disorders? Oh, they're very big, and if you read one of those, oh wow, you'd start to see yourself in a lot of the different diagnoses! "Oh, dear! I didn't know I was bulimic; I didn't know that's what it was called. And look at these other things it says about that; I must be those too. Oh, manic-depressive, yeah; schizophrenic, that's me!" In each of these we'll find something about ourselves, so that's very scary and not empowering at all.

Maybe we felt so out of control that when we hear about a label that describes how out of control we are, for a minute we feel better! "Oh! That explains it; I'm a manic-depressive," or "That explains it, I'm bulimic." We seem to get a handle on the data, because we have our label and somebody else acknowledges the label, and they've agreed to tell us we're that, too. We have our little conspiracy where we all agree on the labels. Not only that, we have a person who will hold us to account for being that label and they'll maybe try to get us to lessen the power of that label on our life.

In order to really understand any of these domains of knowledge, first we need to empower ourselves with open intelligence; otherwise, there is no way to conclusively understand any area of human knowledge; it's absolutely impossible. Whether its psychiatry or genetics or computer science or whatever it is, we cannot take it to the limit unless we take it to the limit from open intelligence, which has no limit.

HOW WE TRULY CONNECT

In all the areas of our life, the special feelings we look for, such as sexual or pleasureful feelings or love feelings or whatever they are, in open intelligence they're always on. Those great feelings are always on, and we start to see that love is something much different than the data we may have accumulated about love. We find love in the depth of our own afflictive states. All the things about ourselves that we've tried to avoid or replace, that's where we find real love. It's very humbling to rely on open intelligence while all these data streams flow on by. Open intelligence is very humbling in a very powerful way. It puts us completely in touch with the reality of who we are and who everyone is.

This is how we connect; this is how all those red dots sprouted up on the map we looked at, with everyone really interested and committed, wanting a change, not wanting to be subjected to all these definitions any longer, wanting to get down to basics and down to the real core of who we are as human beings. A lot of these ideas about who we are as human beings and what human identity is are very old technologies that have nothing to do with us or the way we live today. They're so ingrained in each other and interwoven that it's impossible to really establish their history, but they really have nothing to do with us.

All we can do in terms of seeing ourselves clearly is to rely on open intelligence. We can't progress in our own life or as a society without open intelligence. We really see how powerful it is. We see how everyone is together here in the Balanced View Center, and we have big, big meetings all over the world. We don't have to be sitting here; we could be in Goa, Rishikesh, Dharamsala, in the US, elsewhere in Europe, down in Australia or anywhere in the world. Wherever it might be, there is open intelligence community.

We have a very strong online presence, and we have support available 24/7, so there's never any question about that. People say, "Well, aren't you barraged by all kind of calls and questions?" No, not at all! When we know that support is available, then we're not having to look for it anymore. Just having it available is a huge relief. We empower ourselves as a society in very simple ways, and those ways don't have the same kind of logic that we've previously been using.

When we're talking about ourselves in terms of our labels, then we're boxed into those labels. Say we open up the dictionary and we find 500 labels that apply to us and describe us and they give us a sense of identity. By the power of open intelligence all those labels loosen up, and each label becomes totally spacious. We feel the actual expansion out of ourselves, but including ourselves as well. We don't feel so locked within a skin line. We don't feel, "This is who I am. What makes me who I am is only in here; it isn't anywhere else."

Sometimes that can be kind of scary, but by the power of open intelligence we feel connectivity and power. We feel like we really belong. We are in an open connection—an always on, open connection, a very, very powerful sense of connectivity. Very real, very strong. Anything we want to do in our lives, the power to do it is there. This is very reassuring and is real strength. Real strength is in open intelligence.

One of the areas of relating that is at least of passing interest to most of us is sexuality and sex. To normalize that area of human experience is greatly empowering within human society, because we see how much power we really have. When we are no longer led around by our desires, we see we really do have the power within each one of us individually to control the population naturally and spontaneously—in other words, no pill required. The medicine is open intelligence: the medicine that places all of our actions in the realm of responsibility. We're suddenly able to solve problems that were unsolvable. That's very, very convincing.

Early on in my own life there were many things that I just didn't know what I was going to do about: my feelings of anxiety, or being up and down, or always wanting to accomplish more than I already had. I thought, "I can't live life this way. If this is what life is supposed to be, I'm out of here!" But within me I found an incredible power—the power of open intelligence—and I found that there were many other people interested in that, too. All of these things that seemed unmanageable and that I could never find an answer for no matter where I looked, the answers were found in open intelligence.

Everything was normalized: the sexual education that I needed, the education about respectful relating, living in a culture of gratitude and respect with other people. All this came about due to the power of open intelligence. These aren't idle words; everyone here is evidence of the power of open intelligence. We can all be here together happily, no matter how we're feeling. We feel the support of the group; we know that everyone else here understands our dynamic exactly *as it is*. We no longer need to seek to be understood by other people; we have that understanding ourselves, and it is tacit and certain. That is an incredible power. Without that we will always feel left out; we always feel like we're not understood, and we seek people who will understand us. When we understand ourselves and we make a connection with another human being who looks at things the same way, then we have mutual understanding.

What we are as human beings is very simple, very radical and extremely powerful. If we complicate it, we go out of control. If we simplify it in its radical core power, then all of this comes about. People are able to live together powerfully all over the world really committed to a sane society.

Value Letters from Participants

FIRST SHARE

Thank you so much for every word—spoken and written. There are so many ideas about what it is to be human and what one should have in order to have a good life. It is so empowering to discover how wrong I was in holding to grandiose ideas that didn't bring benefit. By the power of open intelligence all of these ideas faded away. Instead of chasing after certain reflections in the crystal ball, there is instantaneous access to the profound know-how of open intelligence.

The Four Mainstays are my everyday companions. They nourish and clarify my busy and easeful life. Affliction is welcomed and normalized immediately. I am able to experience everything fully and to extract the power from the entire range of phenomena.

This huge open intelligence family is the proof that we as humans are completely simple, kind and powerful. There are no longer enemies in my life—no one to oppose, no one to argue with. Everything is held together in such intimacy, connection and beauty.

I am committed 100% to the Four Mainstays; no one can fool me anymore with confused ideas. From this discernment and open intelligence, my actions and movement in the world are light and effective. Stepping out from the cage of conventional nonsense can be scary at first, but with the support of this huge open intelligence family, there is nothing more exciting and liberating.

SECOND SHARE

In the past few days I have experienced so much joy from the buzz of working together easefully and have been enriched with warmth and love over and over. In the past, before I began relying on open intelligence, some of the volunteers that had assisted me in the kitchen had been fearful and uncomfortable working alongside me, but this year it could not have been more different. Volunteers were specifically requesting to work with me, and together we had a great time. Many of them were interested in my life beyond the kitchen, and there was a keen interest to know what it was that supported me in being much more easygoing, fun and kind than I had been in the past. So, I told them about Great Freedom and then left it up to them to explore it further if they wished.

This demonstrates to me that just in simple things, such as saying "hi" to people, checking in with them or generally being interested in them, that there is the possibility to be of immense benefit. By relying on open intelligence and not on my data, my actions have become more and more enriched with kindness and generosity, and this is fully evident in my conduct.

The more I let all data be as they are, the more relaxed I become, and the more relaxed I become, the more beneficial my actions and conduct are.

THIRD SHARE

During the Fourth Sequence of my first Balanced View Training last year, a whole complex of afflictive states returned. Since my late teenage years I have, from time to time, wrestled with anxiety, depression, suicidal and murderous thoughts and occasional anger outbursts. These negative states, perhaps physiologically induced, could be quite strong, and at times seemingly overwhelming, and would often last intermittently for hours or even days, and then move on, often leaving cheerful buoyancy in their place.

I had tried many things, including much psychotherapy and, at one point, living for several years at a spiritual retreat center. I had learned how to exist with these states; antidotes and replacement worked well enough. Over the years these states were less frequent and more manageable, but still they persisted.

During Sequences Four and Five this circumstantial data package returned very powerfully. My partner and I had been coaching each other to take short moments of open intelligence, and for some reason I was able to take a short moment in the midst of this upsurge, which was so intense at one point I could not see how I could remain in the course. In that moment of relaxation and expansion, the entire complex of data just popped. This was beyond amazing! The force and power of those states were outshone in a single instant of the here-and-now. The mirage was seen as only that.

These data have returned in their spontaneous and unpredictable fashion and can still take over the internal landscape with no apparent open intelligence to be found. Yet, with the ongoing commitment to the Four Mainstays, something profound has changed; the episodes are shorter, less powerful, and are known to be of a different order. Short moments are so much more accessible. The data, when they arise, are now seen only to be data, inseparable from open intelligence itself and are also a beautiful invitation to rely on open intelligence. I am grateful for these particular data, as they have allowed a depth of compassion for so many who have similar ones.

And then there have been my "doubt" datum. From the beginning of my introduction to Great Freedom and Balanced View, I continued intermittently to have strong data like, "I don't really know how to take a short moment; I don't take enough of them; open intelligence is for others; the idea of automatic and continuous open intelligence is a myth, in spite of what I see around me; basically I'm a fraud to even be here at the retreat." This has all shifted dramatically. Open intelligence has become a friend and companion, and short moments happen when and as they do!

For a period of time during this last year and a half, I had found myself letting go of old projects and activities to devote most all of my time to the core competence of open intelligence and working with those who are also resting as open intelligence to spread this historic mission of open intelligence for the benefit of all. That has now somewhat shifted, as I find myself "back in the world" in a much more relaxed manner and seeing that all I do in more conventional settings is a bridge to GF/BV and is a way to reach out to nearly everyone I meet and work with, to introduce them to these world-shifting teachings, and to bring open intelligence's demonstration and skillful means to many of the situations I am in.

Day Three

POTENT QUALITIES AND ACTIVITIES OF HUMAN SOCIETY

The Written Text

The process of indestructible identity of open intelligence is summed up in the empowerment of society with optimal qualities and activities. This takes place through the Four Mainstays of Balanced View:

1. The simple practice of short moments of open intelligence; this is the key button to press for everyone;

2. The Balanced View media unerringly presses the reset button again and again until all of human society is automatically and continuously reset to the potency of open intelligence;

3. The trainers are ultimate friends who completely confirm and evoke our clarity nature;

4. The community is available 24/7 worldwide through a vast communication network comprised of many technologies.

The Four Mainstays elicit the very powerful open intelligence of human society. This text names aspects of our true identity so that these can be easily recognized.

Humanity's open intelligence is spacious, lively, precise and very potent. There is a personal and real sense of expanding ourselves and enriching our environment. It is expansion, enrichment, plenty. We expand constantly, opening purposefully for the benefit of all, and relax into the flow of the beneficial qualities and activities of open intelligence. From the first moment of unending open intelligence, we recognize its stability, permanence and generosity.

In open intelligence the principle of prosperity is extraordinary. Living is very rich and plentiful, and we extend ourselves into the world purposefully, personally, directly, in all ways—mental, emotional, sensorial and otherwise. This is the powerful expansiveness of beneficial intent.

Humanity's mutual open intelligence includes everything in its expansive environment, like the power of vast space contains and pervades countless planets and stars. Open intelligence is settling and potent, openly inviting everything to come in and rest. Open intelligence is openhearted to all, intimate and fierce, wide open to all aspects, seeing them clearly and distinctly and knowing how to act. Stealthy and wrathful, open intelligence instinctively knows how to benefit all.

Open intelligence is fantastically precise and aware; it is tremendously interested and inquisitive. Everything is seen in its own distinct way, with its own particular qualities and characteristics.

Humanity's open intelligence is real openness, a willingness to demonstrate what we have and what we are to everyone. Open intelligence brings to the world a sense of generosity, a sense of promise. In whatever is experienced, there is lots of promise. There is a constant sense of magnetization and spontaneous hospitality. Open intelligence is refreshing and fantastic, no matter what it goes through. It feels good in itself, *as it is*.

Humanity's clarity effortlessly demonstrates qualities and activities that are of benefit to all. It is complete fulfillment of activity without feeling stressed or pushed. It is natural fulfillment in relation to everyday life. The view of open intelligence offers complete effectiveness and efficiency to each datum—the efficient view shining from within each datum. The efficiency of open intelligence fulfills each here-and-now.

In open intelligence, all resentment and confusion are outshone, and the qualities of energy, fulfilling action, and openness remain. The wonderful activity of open intelligence touches everything in its path. Open intelligence sees the possibilities inherent in situations and automatically takes the appropriate course. Open intelligence spontaneously fulfills its nature to be of benefit to all.

Humanity's open intelligence is the foundation. It is the environment that makes possible completely beneficial, prosperous and generous qualities and activities. Its strength is unsurpassable.

Humanity's open intelligence is an environment of all-pervasive spaciousness and completely open potential. It can accommodate anything in its force, just as the vast ocean indivisibly contains all drops of water.

Open intelligence is the assurance that we have everything we need, and there is nothing more to get. Open intelligence in itself is a whole course of action for human society, which enriches it with benefit, prosperity and generosity for all.

By the power of the Four Mainstays, human society enlivens and enacts its potent scope and purpose, expanding human intelligence so that it is co-extensive, interactive and interoperable with the intelligence and power of the multiverse.

Day Three Talk

The key point is short moments of open intelligence, repeated many times, until obvious. In that, there is an increasing sense of mental and emotional stability, of natural ethics, of a balanced view, knowing what to do and how to act, insight into all matters, as well as a consistent power to fulfill beneficial intent. The first moment of open intelligence is the introduction to unending open intelligence which is always spontaneously present. This comes to be recognized through short moments, in other words, uncontrived moments. More and more this becomes the more comprehensive order, rather than the defining of everything with data labels.

The whole way that the trainings are languaged is decided by what people express that they most want to hear. From the time we began, the trainings have been standardized, but the trainings are also customized to tie into whatever is going on with the people who are present.

There is a huge shift that we are undergoing right now from an individual biological identity to an expansive identity that includes the biological identity but is not limited to it. We can see all around us that society is changing radically. That radical change will only sharply accelerate, making what's going on today look primitive. There is a massive momentum underway already that is shifting everything about human society away from individual ideas and into a more expansive view.

A RESOURCE-RICH ENVIRONMENT

The words "awareness," "clarity," "open intelligence" and "the view" are really synonymous. We began using "clarity," "open intelligence" and "the view" because of the grave misunderstanding generally of the word "awareness," which is usually interpreted in a very self-centered way. The actual power of open intelligence is what's important, and that power is extracted in short moments. It's a complete, thorough cut with the past ways of identifying oneself, and in that thorough cut the natural impulse to be of great benefit comes alive.

Initially that great benefit is demonstrated to oneself, because all the data that seemed so real, demanding and commanding are cut through at the root. There's no foolishness any longer about data. Labels are like wisps of air; there are no data that have a nature independent of the power of open intelligence. Open intelligence is the overall empowered view at the basis of all data. It is not something separate, with open intelligence over here and data over there; open intelligence and data are inseparable like the sky and the color blue. We have operated in a completely different fashion—seeing things from an entirely different perspective—but that perspective is cut through at the root, and we no longer believe that data has an independent power. We actually no longer believe or buy into that.

Due to the power of open intelligence, all the things that are considered to be basic needs, that we need so much and that we work so hard to get—such as food, clothing, shelter—come along naturally. We live in a resource-rich environment of open intelligence, a natural intelligence that pervades all dimensions that are imaginable and unimaginable. By the power of open intelligence we are able to really understand that this is the case.

THE NETWORK OF HUMAN INTELLIGENCE

Human intelligence has always been networked from the first time that someone grunted at someone else, and that grunting formed a communication network: somebody communicates and someone else receives the communication. Each human being is an information process among all the information processes of the multiverse. All of those information processes are indivisible in open intelligence; they cannot be divided up. It would be impossible for you, me or anyone else to get out of the multiverse. It's totally impossible; we are forever unavoidably bound together within an expanse of indivisibility. By the power of the Four Mainstays this becomes very clear.

This is so deep and thorough; it goes right to the core of everything. The power is extracted from the data in letting them be as they are, in other words, no longer needing desperately to try to rearrange what one's thoughts or emotions or sensations are in order to feel better. It requires going right to the root—really relying on open intelligence to challenge all assumptions.

In the beginning we may think we're making a choice to recognize open intelligence, but after a while all the chatter about everything just totally subsides. There only is open intelligence recognizing everything and inclusive of everything—the all-comprehensive order, vast, obvious, spontaneously present, completely indivisible. This is the way it actually is.

Just like for you, for me or for anyone else, if you persist in the view of open intelligence, then it will be more obvious, and that will be the case throughout your entire life. There is never a static point of destination that is reached; there is always more and more resources and abundance.

THE POWER THAT IS INNATE IN HUMAN SOCIETY

The current way we live is based on scarcity and stinginess, and our ideas about ourselves really have to do with scarcity and stinginess: that we are not enough, that there is something about our thoughts, emotions, sensations that they need to change, that they need to be other kinds of thoughts, emotions and sensations. We think we need to get in there and manage them and package them into some kind of finite set that will work for us. However, no matter how many human beings have tried to package behavior into an instruction set, it has never worked.

We discover all of a sudden that there is something within us that is already totally secure, but it hasn't been named adequately, and there have not been adequate technological means to communicate it—that's all. We have gone way past our need to rely on certain evolutionary drives that have been running us, such as the drive to acquire, to defend, to bond, even to comprehend. The drive to expand our notion of ourselves subsumes all those other drives in its wake, creating a real power within us.

We really see this power as so evident and alive when we see people coming together and working together effortlessly. This is the way it was since the first day we walked in to the Balanced View Center here in Skåne. We had a retreat a few days after the papers were signed transferring ownership; the retreat was full and everyone was harmoniously working together to empower every aspect of it.

Human society at its root is totally powerful, but the technologies we use to describe identity do not point to that power, and they do not completely confirm that power. We have been thinking that our power is going to come from our special instruction set of data. But then we find there is something greater within every datum: the thriving, beating intelligence of what fuels the datum and really makes it work, and that is its overall perspective and intelligence.

THE STABILITY OF OPEN INTELLIGENCE

In open intelligence we grow to trust ourselves individually and collectively. Open intelligence builds tremendous trust individually; otherwise, we're always hoping for certain data and fearing other data. When we're caught in that cycle of hope and fear, there can be no stability. There is continuous instability based on hope and fear—hoping for certain situations and avoiding others, thinking that certain situations are going to bring us well-being. When we find we don't need to do that anymore, we really relax, we completely relax into our natural power and indestructible stability.

There is a great deal of distinction between being overwrought with data and the stability of open intelligence. The stability of open intelligence is *in* being overwrought with data. Real definitive power is in greatly afflictive states—those states that we don't want to have, that we have never known what to do about. Maybe we do something about them, but then all of a sudden down the road they pop up again. That's because they have only been neutralized. Rearranging data might neutralize the situation but will never give it power, because data has only been dampened down.

When we rely on open intelligence we begin to instinctively recognize that the deep understandings that we've had about our own nature really are true: that deep inside and everywhere we are completely whole and powerful, and we are completely ready to go. We know that no matter what comes along in terms of data, we will be able to handle it.

OPEN INTELLIGENCE IN THE FACE OF DEATH

The power of open intelligence is very convincing and very authoritative—so convincing and authoritative that it rules over everything, including birth and death. By the power of open intelligence while we are alive, at death we see that death is just one more datum. Open intelligence doesn't change; it is unending, and through its power we expand our knowing—the basic power by which we know. That knowing is naturally filled with powerful beneficial expression.

Often when people face death they are afraid of what's happening, and everyone else is afraid, too. They are not quite certain how to handle it. In Great Freedom and Balanced View we have a "Death Training," and the teaching in it is very simple: death is really just like living life.

When anyone goes through the dying process, there are a lot of completely new data that come up because of the circumstances. "Oh, I'm losing my sense of touch; I can't see anymore, I can't taste, I've had my last meal. That's all over now; I won't be making those payments anymore; I've taken my last shower; that car I worked so hard to get—won't be needing that anymore." This can be very shocking if there is no context for it. These things are not talked about openly because there is so much push-back against death and so much seeing of death as some great finality or end.

By the power of being with ourselves as we see all the data appear, endure and disappear, we see that all of it is fueled by open intelligence. This gives us the power to be in any situation, including with someone who is dying, to just let everything be *as it is*. Each situation is completely different, but open intelligence gives dying people—which, by the way, we *all* are—a rich sense of ourselves and of where we are and what's going to come next. Open intelligence is very solid and indestructible. It doesn't need to be put into speech to be communicated.

Open intelligence prepares us for anything. We don't know what is going to happen; we could all hear in five minutes that there is a meteor heading for planet Earth and we are not going to be alive tomorrow. What then? What's everybody going to be thinking about then? We have no idea; however, open intelligence sustains us regardless of circumstances. So, we want that kind of preparedness for our entire life—real stability, no matter what is coming down.

TRAINING IN THE PERSPECTIVE OF OPEN INTELLIGENCE

The wheels of human society are turning in the direction of benefit—profound benefit that will give every human being mental health and physical health, an elective term of life, the ability to upload one's mind and download it into a new body and all kinds of other things. There might be lots of skepticism about this, but these things are actually underway.

There are people working in all kinds of fields who care very much about the well-being of human society. In order to really understand that well-being, open intelligence is essential. Open intelligence is a formidable intelligence that orchestrates all of human society. By tapping into that, we're actually part of that powerful force in a way that is very enduring for us, in a way that really gives us a sense of solidity and indestructibility. Right here, right now, no matter what you're thinking, no matter what your emotion is or what that twitch in your body is, it's all saturated by open intelligence.

We train ourselves to pay attention to the twitch, whether it's a thought, emotion, sensation or other experience. By the power of short moments we train in the open intelligence view rather than in all the data. We're not all wrapped up in the twitch anymore; instead, the twitches are all subsumed in the comprehensive, vast expanse of open intelligence. People all over the world are practicing open intelligence, and that is very good evidence about the way society is going. Very lively, very beneficial, very powerful.

A lot of the ideas we have about identity are so intermingled with religion, and the whole way that we treat our thoughts, emotions, sensations and other experience is really informed by religious beliefs, even if we think we're not religious. It is included in the whole judgment of saying, "This is a good one, this is a bad one, this one's neutral. I've got to get more good ones, get rid of the bad ones. That's what's going to give me power and what's going to give society power." All these are beliefs that really do not apply to a healthy human technology. A healthy human technology sees itself as it is—not according to outmoded beliefs.

We don't want to hold on to all those data; that's why we created the Internet! Online we can let all the data just be out there. We don't want to be managing all our pet data and our pet individual identity anymore. On the Internet we can be anyone we want to be, and we can have bonding and affiliation around that identity. It doesn't matter how berserk it is; there will be somebody who is interested in the same thing. This great spew of data is really a very generous act, and it will all settle down into superb quality of information, superb connectivity and superb power of benefit. The current state of the Internet is just a flash in a pan, like a kid let loose in a candy store.

We don't want to be micromanagers of our data, so we've even created this communication forum to let them all hang out. We don't have to sit on them anymore, and we don't have to spend all of our life's energy trying to pack ourselves into a single identity by which everyone else will know us. This way of living—of having a multi-modal identity—is completely new to most human beings.

CRYSTAL CLEAR

By the power of open intelligence we know whether something is the right action or not without thinking about it. We don't even have to think about it; it's just absolutely clear. Believe me, we're the first ones to know if we have a queasy feeling about one of our actions. "Oh, heading down the wrong course here." Maybe it's the opposite of that: "I'm driven to do this by some kind of impulse beyond my control," and it may feel that way, but it isn't that way.

To give ourselves power means to rely on open intelligence—to rely on the overall view of open intelligence—rather than all the data streams. In that overall view, all of the data settle completely, like a pond that is all stirred up with mud naturally settles when it's left *as it is*. It becomes crystal clear due to simply letting everything settle *as it is*. It doesn't require rearranging all the muck in the pond and trying to get the clear water out of the muddy water.

Our own ability to know our own mind is just like that—crystal clear. All the ideas we have that it's anything other than crystal clear are a fiction, a certain understanding we have had about the way we are. We really need to ask, "Does that way of seeing myself benefit me? Has it brought me mental and emotional stability? What do I know about myself that can ensure my mental and emotional stability in this moment, shape my actions in a way that will not harm me or others and bring conclusive benefit to all of society? What about me isn't all wrapped up in a self-identification process?"

The very act of self-identification is fueled by crystal clear intelligence—the natural intelligence at the basis of everything. It's actually impossible for that intelligence to ever conclusively identify as anything other than itself. It's always spontaneously appearing as everything. This is what we *really* want to count on. Feeling at the whim of emotional waves or different thought structures that have been analyzed in all kinds of different ways by all kinds of members of society really hasn't given us mental and emotional stability. Only open intelligence gives mental and emotional stability.

It's important that our businesses, education and health care—whether it is mental, emotional or physical health care—be informed by open intelligence. The power of open intelligence guides and shows where to go, what to do and how to act. We're all lucky that we know that; we can't be surprised by changes.

Everything, no matter what it is, marvels in its own open intelligence. We get to see that in our own experience. Through short moments, we get to see that everything is resting completely and powerfully in open intelligence, just not resting like a couch potato! Or, even when resting as a couch potato, being totally empowered by open intelligence.

EVERYTHING IS NORMALIZED

Think how long it took us to build up a system of data. None of us were born with all these ways of looking at ourselves; as babies we weren't trying to stop our crying or wetting our diaper! Each of us has been trained in seeing ourselves in a certain way, perhaps because that's all we were exposed to; however, now we see something completely different about ourselves that we didn't know was available to us. This is the real stuff of life, the real basis for going forward. Just this instant of unending open intelligence is an all-conclusive and all-encompassing basis.

When we learn to operate from data, we do that in community with others. Not only are we adopting all the data, everyone else is, too, so that makes it seem like it is normal. "Well, I guess this is just the way it is. Got to feel up and down, up and down. It's just the way humans are." Have you ever felt like that?

In open intelligence everything is normalized. We get to see what normal really is. Data have a fundamental meaning, and that fundamental meaning is the same throughout all data. Their fundamental nature is open intelligence itself shining from within the data—open intelligence, the power to know our own thoughts, emotions and to see them differently. We go from seeing our thoughts and emotions in one way to being released from them completely as a frame of reference. They are fun expressions but nothing to count on—not unless there's completely clear knowledge of their fundamental nature.

What we've done in the past is to classify the data. We set up classes of data, and some of the classes are good and others are bad. We marginalize the data into good and bad, and for our entire life we never really know what it means.

Maybe when we're young we think, "Oh, gee, maybe by the time I'm 21 I'll be an adult." This is what I thought. "The ups and downs of youth will slip behind, and suddenly I will be an adult. I'll know how to operate effectively in the world. There'll be a magic moment, and I'll know what to do about all these thoughts and emotions." I was right; there is a magic moment, and it's right now!

We know this deeply and conclusively from the beginning of our life. We know that about ourselves, and it isn't anything new; it's just that we've been looking in a different direction. When we're introduced to open intelligence, the direction we've been looking in is subsumed and held in an expansive open intelligence—intelligence that has no point from which to view. That's what a balanced view is: no point from which to view. Sometimes adopting one datum, other times adopting another as tools of expression and communication, but not as fundamental statements about reality.

THE TOTAL CONFIRMATION OF YOURSELF

The confirmation of yourself that you feel right here is what open intelligence is. Just that feeling, "I am totally complete exactly as I am. I don't need to change any of my data streams in order to become complete. Just in letting everything be *as it is*, I recognize myself as totally indivisible with the power of the universe. I can rest completely in the indestructibility and indivisibility of everything exactly *as it is*."

No matter what's going on, it rests completely in, of, as and through open intelligence. There is no struggle or effort to get somewhere or to achieve anything. Everything already is *as it is*.

There's no way we can plan the data. They are unpredictable and ceaseless and the flow goes on unendingly. All the ideas about getting to a place of only having certain data where we're the great planners and managers of everything—has it ever happened? Even with all the self-help books, primal scream workshops, Rolfing and politics this way or that—there is no plan for data.

In open intelligence we're assured of a beneficial plan without doing anything. Our foundation is completely firm, completely stable. We're naturally of benefit just by the very act of being. The very basis of our being is beneficial, and as we get more familiar with that, we see ourselves in a new way. We expand our sense of ourselves. The things that used to be so important will change in their degree of importance and in their kind.

A FLAWLESS PERSPECTIVE

When we're all wrapped up in data, we're always trying to find data that will give us some kind of pleasure, even if it's a momentary mental pleasure such as, "I'm going to sit here, and I'm not going to have any thoughts, and then I'm going to feel better." A thought-free state is a datum as well; it is an attempt to get into a special state like bliss that is separate from open intelligence. Those are all just data that'll come and go like everything else. One day we can feel euphoric and think, "I've got it!" Maybe we might even feel that way for weeks or years, and then suddenly something else will come along.

Everything settles in the great bliss of open intelligence. It's just the way it is. Everything's naturally settled already, completely at rest. You're at rest; everything about you is at rest—completely unable to get out of the situation you're in! Even if you chose to end your life, the only thing that would change would be the data, that's all. But open intelligence is always on forever, so there's no getting anything or going anywhere. Everything is relaxed and released in expansive open intelligence.

That sense you have of yourself right here is unending; it can never be destroyed. Initially that may seem new to you, but it's really not so new at all. The sense you have of yourself that is fundamental to you being completely at ease is the real you. There's no need to look for it anymore.

A short moment of open intelligence is a complete confirmation of our nature. Not even short moments are necessary. Many people just listen to the talks, and without anything else they slip naturally into recognizing themselves as they are. What could be easier? No mental effort, no achievement required, no diplomas or tuition fees—always free clarity and open intelligence shining from within whatever is occurring.

Sometimes we can't quite believe that that's the case, only because of the way we've trained ourselves to see things in another way. In short uncontrived moments of open intelligence we become convinced. It seeps into our perspective until we have a flawless perspective just like we have right now—the perspective that knows we're here. *That* is the unfiltered open intelligence perspective—that simple knowing, that simple power to know. It is simple, but very potent, always unfiltered, never colored by anything that comes up within it.

When you look in the mirror you see changes in your physical appearance, and maybe you can see some emotions going on within yourself that are written all over your face and body. However, in that looking you also see what has never changed about you every time you have ever looked in the mirror, whether it's a conscious recognition or not. This complete confirmation of indestructibility is always with us; it matters not how we look, feel or think. It is always present.

When we change perspective, we simply allow stability to take over instability and to see that the stability arises from instability. It's assimilated at the junction of stability and instability, opening up a whole new way of perceiving ourselves and the world. The radical simplicity and power of just this single sealing of each moment is very complete in itself. There's nothing to do. Everything is always sealed by the intelligence at the basis.

Value Letters from Participants

The introduction to open intelligence was so simple for me to grasp, and I took it step by step. When I was first introduced to open intelligence a few years ago, I didn't understand much English, and it was hard for me to read or speak it. It was strong data stream for me, but I knew that I wanted to learn everything about gaining confidence in open intelligence, because it was simple and beautiful and I could see the results every day.

Right in the beginning I was encouraged by the trainer to stay and to participate in the teaching and to write a letter and read the text aloud. I felt so disturbed, uncomfortable, stupid, slow and limited, but every day I read my value letter anyway. Through the support of the teaching and the trainers I saw that my data need not be my focus. I could understand that there was nothing wrong with not speaking English well, and just by seeing that, everything relaxed. This is only one example of their support and what it meant to me; it showed me that I'm not limited at all by my data, and I'm able to face them completely. It was very empowering.

I recognize how stable I am, regardless of what data are appearing. From the beginning my trainer never saw me as my data. With her encouragement and love I came to the point where I could see myself as she saw me—as a powerful expression of open intelligence and not as my data!

SECOND SHARE

I can't believe that I am so lucky to be sitting here with you and this wonderful group of people. I am so inspired and empowered. Thank you so much.

Before the "thorough blow of open intelligence" I was confused as to why I would sometimes feel extremely happy, capable and connected and sometimes feel the extreme opposite. I couldn't figure out the reason behind all my ups and downs. I accumulated incomplete knowledge that tried to explain the way things are in very nice words and concepts, and it felt better than the usual stuff, but deep inside I felt limited and bewildered. I recognized the futility and impotency of everything that I held to so dearly and had built my entire life upon.

When I was introduced to open intelligence, all my buttons were pushed, but the introduction and key instructions day after day expanded my view dramatically. I never felt so alive. I realized that I had always been committed to open intelligence and well-being above all else, but I just didn't understand what open intelligence and well-being really were. Once I understood them, I wanted to take it all the way. My aspiration for open intelligence met with this clear instruction, and it was a lucky meeting!

The chaos and pain that I experience daily is a great driving force for me to rely on open intelligence and to be courageous enough to stand tall in the midst of everything. Open intelligence is so simple, direct and powerful. I am excited by the on-going unfolding of my own strengths, gifts and talents and those of my clear and dear friends.

The value of the open intelligence blast is unimaginable. A month ago I bought a large four-wheeled suitcase; having it means that I am immediately ready to go wherever I'm needed and to do whatever is needed; plus, now I can do it with a bit more style!

Thank you, Candice for the blast that blows open the here-and-now. You have answered all my questions—even the ones I have not asked yet.

THIRD SHARE

Ten months ago I didn't have any idea that this Balanced View movement existed. In September last year a therapist I used to go to told me that there was a very good website with free videos to watch. Since this was a person I trusted deeply, I went to the website and watched the videos on the Basics Page, and I realized that this was something completely different. Someone was describing how things actually are, not like an idea or a theory where you can reject some parts and agree with others, but describing how things are in a simple and accessible way.

Since then I've come back more and more to the web site, not always understanding everything that's being said, but knowing that this is it. A month after seeing the web site I went to an open meeting in a city half an hour from where I live in Sweden. I found that what they were saying at the open meeting was confirming what I had heard from the talks on the web site. The people there in the meeting were very inspiring; they were shining and so kind and open.

A couple of months later I did the Basic Clarity training and then the Twelve Empowerments, and this was an incredible way to come closer to the Four Mainstays—reading the teachings for myself and together with the others, listening to the teacher's comments and being able to ask questions and also to share this experience of relying on open intelligence with other human beings.

I would also really like to thank the people who have done the participants' shares. It has been so helpful to me to watch these videos; through your shares of how your life was like before you met the teaching and then what has happened since, I feel stronger knowing how many people are just like me.

Accompanying me on this journey has been my dear younger sister. After watching some of the videos on the web site, I told her about it and she also became interested in the teaching. Now we are resting together, supporting each other every day in who we are. My sister has always been so special to me, and I've always wanted the best for her, and now I can watch her grow stronger and stronger as each day goes by. I would do anything for her, and to realize that's it it's as easy as recognizing the already present open intelligence is such a wonderful feeling.

She has been the light in my life, the reason not to kill myself, even though those thoughts had arisen. Now there are no words to explain how thankful I am for her, for this teaching and for everyone who is making reliance on open intelligence the core in their lives. I had felt before like such a failure for not being able to help my sister when she'd gone through the same things as I had. Being the older sister, I saw that as my responsibility. But being here with the community, I see that helping one another is not a matter of someone fixing someone else.

Once again I feel excitement in my life; I feel alive and like anything can happen. We can create all kinds of things in this world; living with the Four Mainstays in this retreat makes me believe that in a deep and convincing way. Before coming to this retreat, phrases like "a better world" were just words, but now seeing it before my very eyes I'm more and more convinced. I know this is what I've been looking for, and what everyone else is looking for.

Day Four

KEY INSTRUCTIONS IN BENEFICIAL OPEN INTELLIGENCE

The Written Text

Key instructions elicit potent the benefit of open intelligence. Open intelligence and benefit are inseparable like a crystal ball and its luminosity.

Open intelligence deals not with the name tags of data but with its own innate perfection and spontaneous generosity. Name tags applied to the here-and-now are outshone by beneficial open intelligence.

The liveliness of open intelligence is trained up by pressing key buttons provided by open intelligence itself. These key instructions completely confirm the obviousness of open intelligence in all data, expanding the power of beneficial open intelligence, infinitely.

The potent intelligence of clarity is reflected in the liveliness of the here-and-now spontaneously self-releasing in tremendous benefit to all. Generosity and prosperity are the outpouring of open intelligence. Spontaneously beneficial, generous, prosperous open intelligence is set free to benefit human society and the world. The generosity of open intelligence is the basis of all the gifts expressed by body, speech, mind, qualities and activities. Open intelligence is required to bring these gifts to life. Open intelligence opens the expansive treasury of benefit, generosity and prosperity.

The words, sounds and images of the here-and-now express innate open intelligence, so there is nowhere else to look. The pure logic of the here-and-now is thoroughly perfect, all-powerful complete confirmation of the total stability at the basis of reality.

Look! Look! The here-and-now beneficially slips in and out on its own. Benefit, prosperity and generosity are the natural state of collaborative open intelligence.

Sounds are the song of pervasive open intelligence announcing itself. The natural spontaneity of the here-and-now is the ultimate identity, the nectar of meaning—saturated beneficial potency.

Open intelligence is the only fundamental basis of identity. In open intelligence, you carry on, remaining as you are, strong and stable. There is no other identity to be had. The prime imperative of open intelligence is indestructible uncontrived benefit.

The here-and-now has never been before and will never be again. The here-and-now cannot be captured or examined by any mechanism. Yet each transparent here-and-now is super-complete, totally present in open intelligence. Open intelligence is the fundamental identity of anything or anyone. Each moment of open intelligence is the greatest investment deposit to be made by anyone during any moment of life. This investment alone will return riches beyond wildest imagination.

Know open intelligence as yourself—your sole, indestructible, reliable identity. Its power to consistently fulfill beneficial intent is your own. All human viewpoints are liberated in a mass of open intelligence settling deeply into human society. There is no distinction between open intelligence and human intelligence.

So utterly simple, open intelligence is the embodiment of benefit, prosperity and generosity.

Day Four Talk

When we grow up in human culture today, we learn all kinds of things about identity. We learn that we have a personality, and we learn about different psychological types. Maybe we have a diagnostic and statistical manual with thousands of ways of describing human behavior. However, when we're confronted with open intelligence-identity, we're confronted with completely cutting through the whole idea of a human being as a pathological individual. The diagnostic and statistical manual and other means of describing personality types are all based on lessening pathology rather than creating spontaneous, powerful beneficial open intelligence. These two ways of looking at human beings are very, very different.

All of human culture to this point in time has been built on seeing human beings as pathological—needing to be fixed and corrected—and we spend our whole lives in a process of trying to correct ourselves, but never being able to do that. We have learned that the positive, negative and neutral data are the sole substance of our identity. Even if we learn something else that might be spiritual, religious, metaphysical or philosophical in nature, we learn that whatever that perfect thing is, it is separate from us. We learn that it's ruling over us in some way and that it's an entirely different kind of being that has nothing to do with us and which is making judgments about us. We are the poor pitiful ones who are overcome with pathologies. This is the basic means of identification that human culture has used up to this point: to address ourselves as statements of imperfection.

When we're introduced to open intelligence, we find within ourselves and immediately within everything an expanse that has nothing to do with imperfection. It subsumes imperfection, in other words, it's a more comprehensive order, a more comprehensive intelligence than parsing and nuancing everything into positive, negative and neutral. We completely set aside that old intelligence. We subsume it in the power of a comprehensive order that is so many orders of magnitude greater than parsing and nuancing data.

In this comprehensive order, all data are equally a source of the powerful intelligence and have nothing to do with defining reality. It doesn't matter if they're good ones or bad ones, whatever they are, the data have nothing to do with defining reality. It is open intelligence itself—totally clear, luminous and illuminating—that is the basic intelligence. It is a matter of using words as simple tools to communicate its message, and its message is a message of the natural perfection of nature itself, including human nature. It is an actual science, where you can test it in the laboratory of yourself and see the results. It is not just a bunch of words that point to something far off and remote, but is something tested in your own experience that you find has a power over all the pathologies you thought you had.

All these pathological conditionings have been adopted, and just as easily they can be dispensed. It's much easier to dispense them than to hang on to them. Hanging on to them only brings decrease in energy, increasing tiredness, fatigue, old aging and death, where death is seen as a threat and foe instead of the greatest welcoming force that one could ever be presented with. These are all complete perversions of what identity is. To think of ourselves as being pathological is perverse.

When we simply settle in to the ease of what we actually are, it's wonderful and comfortable, and at the same time it is a complete confrontation to everything we have ever believed about ourselves. We get to see it all nakedly for the first time. We see that data pose no threat. Whether they are good or bad, they pose no threat. They are open intelligence itself that are the basis of intelligence—always on, always powerful, always clear. It may take a while to get the hang of it, but in the meantime, so what? Whatever thought, emotion, sensation or experience you're having—whatever datum is arising—rely on open intelligence rather than emphasizing the data. This is the greatest healing act and the greatest miracle that will ever occur for you or for anyone else.

WHAT TO DO WITH YOUR LIFE

If you're wondering what to do with your life, just get down with open intelligence and then you'll know what to do. Maybe the option you're involved in right now won't be an option anymore. By the power of open intelligence you find out that there are a lot of things you absolutely will not do any longer. You will no longer debase yourself, and you will not debase others.

How do you find that out? You stop putting yourself through the ringer over every single data stream that you have, toiling over what to do with all of these data. You just stop; you won't do it anymore. My advice would be that you just go to any lengths to have that as your primary project, because you can't go wrong there.

Even, say, if you quit your job and you had no source of income because you decided, "This job isn't a place where it's comfortable for me to practice open intelligence," that would be fine and everything would turn out all right. I've done it myself and it posed no threat. I went completely and totally against everything my parents and all of society told me to do with the skills I have. Where did I get that courage? I got it from the power of open intelligence.

My parents wanted me to live a certain way, my husband wanted me to live a certain way, and I thought my children wanted me to live a certain way. I did not do that. Why? Because of the power of open intelligence I could see how to be of benefit to all. I could see how to be a true participant in healthy human society, beyond all the fixed frameworks or beliefs for myself that others had given me and that I had taken on. I just stopped. I took the open intelligence trip, and I let that intelligence soak into every single aspect of my life. I ended up doing a lot of things in my life that I never dreamt possible, like sitting here speaking in front of a large group of people!

GOING BEYOND THE USUAL FRAMEWORKS

The power of open intelligence is very, very great. It doesn't need any current frameworks or ideas to get things done. For example, when we started our website, we put up a single page, and the idea was, "Okay, there's our website. Now everyone else is going to let us know what they want on the website." We didn't have to have a great plan. We just waited to hear from everyone, "What do you want to contribute to the website? What kinds of things do you want to see on the website?"

We had to face all kinds of things, such as what the content on the website would cost people. That was easy; it would be free. So, all the media is free. It's wasn't like, "You listen to a little bit and, whoops, all of a sudden you have to buy it." Everything is free, and there is lots of it. All of this came about through the contributions of time and/or financial resources from many people. That fantastic website we have was built by participants. All the media that are provided were brought about by participants worldwide. This is the way open intelligence works. It's an expanse of open generosity.

This sort of model completely goes against everything we've learned about money and how we think about ourselves in regard to money. We learn about money that, well, it's a special thing. First of all you've got to find out how to get it. Let's say you're a little kid and you have no money; you've got to get it from somewhere, so you've either got to get an allowance from your caregivers or you've got to get a job. Then, once you get money, you've got to keep it—at least long enough to pay for the roof over your head or the one-fourth cup of lentils a day that you're stirring in your pot that you get to eat from your earnings. Many people live like this.

Then you've got to get some more money. You've got to keep this whole thing going. If you have enough, then maybe you want to still get more anyway so you'll have more than enough. This keeps going on and on until money is one of the first things you think about in life, and it's the last thing—adopting money as a special power and force, living in a state of scarcity and stinginess and being afraid. "What about my money? What am I going to do if I don't have enough? If I don't have money, then I might be pushing a shopping cart on the street."

We have to get real about the structures we've set up for ourselves in the world. They do not work and they will never work, because they are based on the wrong fundamental principal. Our intelligence, just *as it is*, is one of generosity and not one of scarcity and stinginess. If we live in a mode of scarcity and stinginess, that's exactly what we'll have. If we live in the mode of open intelligence, more and more our heart will open in generosity, to the degree that we will never even have to think about money—how to get it, when to get it, where to get it. All the resources flow naturally in open intelligence. Open intelligence is humanity's greatest natural resource, and we're just beginning to mine it. It's an infinite resource; it never stops giving. It tells us exactly what to do in each area of life.

CHANGING THE WAY WE LOOK AT OURSELVES

The whole area of mental instability is a problem that has not been solved in the four million years of the human race. There never has been a tool or a technology that gives human beings complete mental and emotional stability. Now due to the power of open intelligence there is such a tool. It is a simple tool to share with one another, radical and powerful, that changes our whole way of looking at ourselves and looking at the world. It not only changes our mental and emotional instability to complete stability, but then with the power of a lively intelligence, we're able to see how to change the world in marvelous, miraculous ways that have never existed before.

What a relief to stop living life as though it were the Judgment Day! These metaphors we learn, like Judgment Day, become very ingrained in the way we think about ourselves. No matter where we live, the whole idea of human imperfection has saturated all of our institutions—hospitals, prisons, institutions of education, politics, the criminal justice system. They're all saturated with the view that human beings are imperfect creatures who basically have no hope; all we can do is try to keep the bad ones away from the good ones. These ideas are based on ideas that no longer work and have never really worked.

We have to use the power of our own body and mind to come to a conclusion about this, and we come to a conclusion about it in a very personal way. Within ourselves we see that we have an incredible power that we didn't know we had. The whole project of building up a self-identity is just no longer important. Self-referencing is not an issue. Whether one is referencing self or no self, who cares? I don't.

Every single time we try to control our data we're actively pushing open intelligence away. Open intelligence can't jump up and say, "Here I am!" It's a disempowering act to try to constantly be regulating all the data. Some people have way more afflictive states than others, but it does not matter. The only solution is to train in simple open intelligence.

Even people who are so mentally ill that they need to be in a hospital are greatly benefitted by the power of open intelligence. There are more and more people working in this way, including right here in Sweden: using no medications even with the most psychiatrically ill whether they're in the hospital or out of the hospital. These innovators are totally committed to a way of healing people that doesn't involve these extreme methods. We can change our society by taking a look at who we really are and making a commitment to that, and not copping out.

DEEPLY CARING FOR EACH OTHER

If we have an intimate relationship with another person, we may see all kinds of things come up which we never saw about ourselves before, and our buttons really start getting pushed. Open intelligence is the only way to sustain a relationship; otherwise, it'll be a painful experience, usually one where, after a while, we try to make it all right just because we've been hanging out together for so long. Basically it's totally painful in a way that can't be offered any remit, but by the power of open intelligence our life as an individual and our relationships are enriched.

Many times when people hear about open intelligence, they make it into a new datum. "Now I'm going to try to stay in the open intelligence-datum," but there *isn't* an open intelligence-datum. Open intelligence is in all data. The good things you think about yourself and the bad things and the things that you never think about and do automatically, like brushing your teeth or tying your shoes, open intelligence shows up as the fuel for all of that. By just hanging out it becomes clear that that's the case. There isn't anywhere to go.

The battle is over; the Judgment Day has come and gone. There is no need to spend every day judging all your thoughts, emotions and sensations. You can just relax. They're the power and the fuel of open intelligence. Just like a sponge soaks up water, open intelligence soaks up all the data.

Now, feeling an open intelligence-connection with other people is a matter of simply getting used to it. At first you might think, "Oh, now I feel separation; now I don't feel like I'm connected. Oh, now I do! Am I too connected?" but all these are merely data. They'll all settle out and then you'll be hanging out with everybody else. That's the way I feel: just hanging out with everybody else. To be connected in that way is what human health is really about. It's to be connected in that way, instead of being frantically obsessive over your own data and trying to change other people's data in order to make your data more comfortable. That is a lot of work!

Instead of that game plan, everyone is relaxed in open intelligence and completely connected. No data to change here. I don't have to change any of your data to make my data more comfortable, so we can just hang out in total, blazing power. I don't have to try to figure you out, because I've figured myself out. You know what I need, I know what you need, and I can support you in doing that, just like you support me. That makes relationship totally simple and easy, very compelling and profound.

If you're together with someone and you've been together for a long time, by relying on open intelligence you will without a doubt notice a much greater ease in the relationship. All the prepackaged ideas about who the other person is, what they're up to, who you are, what you're up to—all that just settles down in open intelligence-companionship.

For anyone committed to open intelligence, if you don't have a partner and you're looking for one, I'd suggest you come together with someone else who's committed to open intelligence; otherwise, it'll be a lot of work. It is a lot easier if you're hanging out with someone who's made the open intelligence-commitment. Then you know from the get-go that that person really knows you, and they know where you're coming from; they're not going to try to get you to change your data. You see that somehow the two of you together are going to be able to be very beneficial, and so that's what your whole life is about—bringing joy to each other in the fun of creation and excitement. Really, really deeply caring for each other, rather than constantly trying to change each other's data.

BEING A PARENT

The choice to have a child is an extremely serious one for someone who is committed to open intelligence. Here's the first helpful advice for those who want to be parents: you never know which one you're going to get! Each parent dreams of having the perfect child, but it's very rare that that happens. Whatever you have, that's what you've got, and once you have them, that's it for as long as you live. No matter what you think of them, they're yours. You cannot bludgeon them into open intelligence. They will either pick up on open intelligence through your example or they won't. Here again you have another situation where you may need to spend your whole life with a person who does not have a commitment to open intelligence.

If your child is not interested in open intelligence, that means that while you continue to live as an example of it, you will need to provide your child a way to deal with their life. You are going to have to train your child in antidotes that you do not use yourself in order to live their life in a somewhat peaceable way. If you teach your child to focus on positive antidotes—replacing negative data with positive data—they might have a little bit of a better life than if they were indulging data all the time. "Relying on open intelligence" or "utilizing antidotes"—these are the only two ways to go really, which makes parenting very simple. Either way, parenting is a fulltime commitment. It is complete responsibility for the well-being of another human being and a complete commitment to showing that other human being how to live.

Children need structure. That's the most important thing a parent can give a child: structure and the ability to make decisions from the beginning of their lives. You can teach a baby to make decisions and to become a good decision-maker just by not putting a toy into one hand or the other. You hold the toy and let them choose how to grab it. This is the way to empower babies from the get-go. Let them choose what they're going to drink; do they want juice or do they want milk—let them choose which one.

This is what it is to be a parent: to put structures together so children have a very strong core that they can live from for the rest of their lives without being in lifelong dependence on you. A lot of people today think that letting kids run wild doing whatever they want is the way to raise children, but it's not. That will bring about a person who cannot take care of themselves. Show them how powerful they are; from the beginning let them do household tasks. Don't do everything for them; instead, show them that they're capable. They can make their own school lunch, and they can have their list of activities where they are contributing to the caretaking of the home you all share.

All of this is integrated from the very beginning. If that isn't done, they'll expect you to be doing for them for the rest of their lives, and they'll expect you to be taking care of them. At some point or another this very real conversation of parameters will have to arise. You will need to say, "Well, you're an adult now, and even though I may not have been acting like that and you may not either, now is the time to put some parameters together." These parameters are the core of good relationship, they really are. No matter where you are in your parenting, you can change your relationship with your child.

When I was a new mother, I wanted to be perfect and do everything right. Not only was I looking at my own data, I was trying to decide how my data were going to affect my kids, and this is a very important concern. If you plan to be a parent, you can plan to devote a great deal of your energy to that. Even if you have a job, you'll be thinking about your children. This is the reality of parenting.

A lot of time we have a lot of data that govern whether we become a parent or not. In fact, most of us have had our children based on data and not on open intelligence. There are strong data such as, "I won't be a total woman unless I have a child." The opposite could also be true: "I don't want a child," and many people feel that way, but they feel compelled by society to have a child. Now we have an opportunity for a world of people to have children based on commitment to open intelligence rather than data.

There are no societal rules requiring people to have children. It's a biological impulse, a drive, but open intelligence has complete dominion over all biological impulses. There's no need to carry out a biological impulse. Any impulse is just as clear and pure and illuminated by open intelligence as anything else. Really look at yourself very deeply, and if you want to have a child, talk to your trainer about it in depth, rather than just going off and doing something without proper consideration. It is best to be completely settled into open intelligence before even thinking about having a child. That needs to be the primary commitment.

I can just tell this about myself: if I did not rely on open intelligence, I would be a real busybody in my kids' lives! Do you know what a busybody is? Meddling, getting in there showing them how to do things, telling them what to do. I have eight grandchildren too, so I'd have a lot of people to tell what to do! But now, I don't have to do any of that. I can watch them enjoy their life and hang out with them once in a while.

When they were growing up and they would ask me for advice I would say, "What do you think?" I learned that this was the best answer; it showed them how to really look into what they think and what their own resources are to respond to situations. They'd say what they thought, and I would say, "That sounds good; you're a good decision maker." That's the kind of advice I give. They turned out great, and I feel very blessed and lucky every day because they are both totally incredibly beautiful men with clear heads and completely compassionate hearts, totally responsible leaders and friends.

RELATIONSHIP WITH THE TRAINER

Ideally, the relationship with the trainer is a lifelong relationship, and the deepening of the relationship with the trainer is in allowing them to know you completely through contact with them. Even though initially you may have needed something from them, at some point you might want to give something back—for instance asking them how you could help them in some way. They may decide they have a project that's perfect just for you, and they'll ask you what you'd like to do. Then all of a sudden you're going to start finding out all kinds of new things from this relationship with the trainer.

This is really what community is all about: all of these people here connecting to grow this worldwide community. There are many service projects for giving generously of your time and your other resources. This is a wonderful, wonderful way to live life. Every single person can provide some kind of giving to the worldwide network and community. No matter what your skills are, there's something really special about you that has just the right place.

All that is required is that, if you have a suggestion you also have a plan for implementing that suggestion and that you're willing to carry it out. Those are the kinds of suggestions we read. We get all kinds of suggestions, but unless they're backed up with a plan of action and the resources to actually bring it about, then we don't read that suggestion. In that simple way— just being solution-oriented and asking for people to provide solutions—all of this has come about. It's really effective, and it really works.

Having a relationship with a trainer helps pull your covers! The trainer can point out things to you that you wouldn't see otherwise. It doesn't mean that you always have to come to the trainer and say, "Oh, I've got this and that problem." Just in the flow of service all these things are seen. The relationship with the trainer is a fortunate relationship, and I would strongly suggest that you do everything possible to hook up and really make a connection.

If you receive a service project from the trainer, and it seems like something you can't possibly do, in the very act of showing yourself your power to do whatever it is, it will completely un-ravel thousands of data. Running on the fuel of open intelligence, you see that you're capable to do all kinds of things you never dreamt of doing.

OPEN MEETINGS IN YOUR LOCAL COMMUNITY

When you have open meetings in your local community, it's really important that the focus of those meetings be open intelligence. If the focus is anything else, you won't be helping yourself and you won't be helping anyone else. This is how over 7,600 cities have open intelligence commitments: it's because everyone knows that when they come to an open meeting the sole purpose of that meeting is open intelligence. It isn't anything else.

If you want to have another meeting related to your group, like a business meeting or about how or where to have a later meeting, separate that out from the open meeting. Then if you do have a business meeting, let it be fully business-oriented, where you are there to *solve* particular problems and not just *talk* about problems.

If your local group has a suggestion, you can show up and let the management team know what your suggestion is, but it does not mean your suggestion will be acted on. It's the world group that decides about the suggestions, not any one individual group. There's no one individual group or person running the show. Everyone deciding together is how it comes about.

What the most people want, that's what we do. Most people wanted many downloads, so that's what we gave them. That's what works best. People just liked it that way, and we don't even have to ask why; we just responded to what they asked for. Some people wanted a smaller selection of more specific downloads, so we made "The Basics Page," which is enough for anyone. Something for everyone: we know how to do it and we do it together. This makes it simple.

Value Letters from Participants

FIRST SHARE

Before the Mainstays were a part of my life, I felt like life was a hall of smoke and mirrors with the walls always seeming to cave inward and never outward. My role models were rather coarse, critical, judgmental and snobbish. Emotions were a sign of weakness as was needing or asking for help. If you weren't the best at whatever you did, you were basically not much of anything.

Paradoxically though, by conventional standards it was a good life: the right education, the right job, the right husband, the kids, the car, the house, the money but so what…there had to be something more to it than this, right?

With reliance on the Four Mainstays I can trust again. I am completely open, relational, non-judgmental, filled with love, appreciation and gratitude for people and things I didn't really even notice before, and I am filled with a humble respect for it all. There is no more striving and effort. There is no need to show up in a certain way, there is no more harsh criticism of myself or others, and I have a natural confidence that comes from a recognizable and demonstrable stability and skillfulness. It is this that I rely on. From this reliance data are completely de-energized.

Like the refection in a pond, we are a microcosm of something much larger, and my life is a complete refection of human society as a whole. How can it be any different? We are all just seedlings of open intelligence dropping ourselves wherever we are and leaving behind a beautiful garden of open intelligence for all to nurture themselves. It really is up to each of us to make this incredible choice for ourselves.

Life is good, really good, in a way that it never could be before. This is my driving force for sharing this training with others. No smoke and mirrors anymore, just a clear reality provided by the power of relying on the Four Mainstays and lived out very directly in my own circumstantial walk. Words will never be enough to express my love and gratitude and appreciation. So today I am just honored and humbled by it all.

SECOND SHARE

The importance of key instructions is that they are steeped in open intelligence, and so they are very purposeful in allowing us to see through old habitual patterns of limitation, imperfection and scarcity. What I particularly enjoy about the instructions is that they have the single purpose of complete empowerment— empowering one's own recognition of open intelligence in order to empower others. It is hard to choose my favorite instructions, but I do remember a few as having significant importance to me.

• The first was: "Just show up." No need to do anything else but show up with an open and willing disposition, give yourself three months and see what happens. What do you have to lose? This allowed me the wiggle room I needed to do my own point of view dance.

• The second was: "Sarcasm is the lowest form of humor and a total affront to yourself and others." I listened to the talks on sarcasm as was suggested, transcribed them and then watched a lifetime of data around that type of relating come to the fore and resolve all at once!

• The third was: "Rest and get busy. There are many mountains to climb, but you really want to expend your energy on the one that is going to surpass all others." This provided me the opportunity to take on each and every service position that was offered so that I could stay focused and surrounded by others committed to open intelligence.

• The fourth was: "You are in total control of the life you live. If you know what you are looking for and *what's looking*, then believe me, your life can be anything you want it to be." I would have never believed that from anyone else, but the brilliant clarity of the statement went right through me. I knew it was right there for the taking, if I allowed it to be that way.

• The fifth was: "Don't try and hide out among many people; choose a trainer/service mentor and allow that person to really know you." From that a multitude of instructions came informally and formally through many different ways: sometimes a look, sometimes a hand on my shoulder, sometimes a spoken word and sometimes nothing at all, but no matter how it was offered, the space of open intelligence shone forth brilliantly allowing me to see exactly what was needed.

And lastly, "Just look at your own experience and confirm that it is this way for you." This is the most gentle, compassionate and loving of them all. Nothing to do but allow the gradual fruits of open intelligence to take hold in your life.

From following these instructions I have opened myself up to riding this unscripted wave of natural responsiveness, generosity, benefit and prosperity that is a life based in open intelligence. These riches keep coming and coming, all from this single commitment to show-up and stay put.

I just look at the incredible changes that have unfolded for me in such a short period of time, and I know that these have to be the real deal because they are my experiences and not someone else's. This is real assurance. WOW! Thank you, thank you, thank you.

Day Five

THE MUTUAL POWER OF OPEN INTELLIGENCE

The Written Text

In open intelligence, tremendous benefit is freely given and received. Data are the actual fulfillment of open intelligence's nature, decisively cutting through all notions of lack. The here-and-now is *as it is*—the gift of open intelligence. By the power of short moments, all woes are outshone, first individually and then collectively. This is our power and strength, the great shining forth of open intelligence's pervasive beneficial nature. Each datum is the birth of great bliss, a wide open generosity that provides specially for everyone, without exception, in all data.

All data flow on by, and open intelligence is shining forth from within all, welcoming all as its natural treasury, its beneficial power and energy.

Just as space presents a 100% commitment to receiving the liveliness of everything within it, so open intelligence is 100% committed to the here-and-now. Open intelligence's view is forever seamless, flawless and potent within all data. Space has no resistance to filling itself with mirage-like here-and-now, vanishing naturally without a trace into the continuity of open intelligence's care. Each here-and-now is the exclamation of open intelligence.

The open-intelligence view is instinctively recognized—a steady instantaneous recognition of the way things actually are.

Likewise, in openly allowing data to be as they are, they turn into the potency of humanity's own stable beneficial mind, body, speech, qualities and activities. Rather than emphasizing any given datum, we simply let everything be *as it is*. Discovered shining forth from within data is open intelligence's great power and benefit! What a wondrous marvel this is! By profound short moments, we open to very powerful intelligence that is inaccessible when relying on data.

Money data are the call of open intelligence, calling us to untold riches—not to work harder to make more money. By letting the money data be as it is, the door to the open intelligence-treasury opens up and its all-providing energy replaces the exhaustion of making money and accumulating things. Instead, super-beneficial body, speech, mind, qualities and activities are filled with open intelligence's potency devoted to all, giving everything that is required without limit or restriction. The surety of open intelligence replaces the constant mental muttering about money. In simultaneous receiving and giving, we are released from a constant sense of lack and imperfection into prosperity and infinite generosity.

In this way, even the data about sickness, aging and death are the vivid potency of all-soothing, extremely potent open intelligence, like the force of the ocean is inseparable from the ocean itself.

Each datum is the song of open intelligence calling to itself, the potent inseparability of all things.

By the mutual open intelligence power we instinctively know how to be mentally and emotionally stable and powerful together. Right now, we know how to build a just and sane society with resources for all. We see it right here. Open intelligence shows us very personally that all resources are already available, infinitely, simply by relying on open intelligence. Open intelligence is the greatest natural resource, and its wealth of offerings continuously gives more and more. The more power that is extracted from open intelligence, the more it has to offer.

Open intelligence and service are inseparable—open intelligence in service, service in open intelligence—the first of the essential Four Mainstays. In each moment of open intelligence, we serve ourselves and all beings completely.

In allowing data—the here-and-now—to be as they are, we relax within all our own data; thus, we open to the great mutuality of open intelligence and data, the potent heart of all relating. Without its data, open intelligence would not be.

Data are the power of open intelligence. When a datum is instinctively recognized *as it is*, there is no restriction of the power of open intelligence, and it increases in potency each moment. Although this potency may be subtle at first, open intelligence power increases each and every moment when we are committed to its obviousness. We carry on, head held high, counting on open intelligence, as it becomes obvious that it is the ruler of all we behold. This is the only means of extracting the power from humanity's data.

When all data are allowed to be as they are, mutually we see that in each moment we are the vast, lively intelligence of open intelligence containing all data, not just our own. Each moment of open intelligence is simultaneously giving and receiving all data of the here-and-now, all at once, seamlessly, like the powerful ocean gives and receives all drops of water. Without drops of water, the great force of the ocean would not be; without data, open intelligence would not be. In open intelligence, all data whatsoever is simultaneously received and given in a great flow of benefit.

All negativity of all kinds, individual and collective, is overcome, exhausted and outshone by the uncontrived means of instinctive clarity. Open intelligence in the current data unleashes the greatest power and natural resource in the world for the benefit and enjoyment of all.

The Four Mainstays of open intelligence are the foremost instruction, the education informing all others, the one that is core in every way, that comes out at the front of all other kinds of education, the one that actually has the ability to get right into our body, speech, mind, qualities and activities and unlock the power to benefit for all.

Day Five Talk

Words can be a temporary diversion or even a distraction—a moment of entertainment or something to ponder on once in a while. Or, they can be the words that enter in and forever change the body, speech, mind, qualities and activities of the people in the audience, a pure connection that is the pure connectivity of great mutuality of everyone together in great open intelligence. There's a distinction between those kinds of words and the words of entertainment or information.

What kind of connection do you want to make? This is true for everyone; we can go on and on our entire lives blabbing away about things, or we can enter into true connection, where every word we speak is imbued with the resonance that directly enters in. The words have an effect far beyond the syllables; they have a permanent resonance that from that moment on never goes away. One actually lives in that open resonance that had maybe been shut down.

PANORAMIC VISTA

We all feel a little bit shy to open our mouths; some of us might feel like we're going to the guillotine if we have to get up and talk in front of a crowd! I have a friend who's a famous actress, and she says that performers are all nervous, no matter how famous they are. Some people vomit one bucket before a performance and some are two-bucket people!

An actor on stage or in film has to have complete authority over the role they're portraying. There can't even be a slight veering off course, and it has to be dead-on every time, or everyone will know it. Plus, when they get up there, they know that no one in that audience cares what kind of day they've had. Not only that, everyone in the audience wants the actor to perform just for them—no matter what's happened with the actor at home with the girlfriend, the boyfriend, the mother, the father, the friends.

If we get up in front of other people and we have nothing to prove—or if in any interaction we have nothing to prove—

where everything just totally is *as it is*, then there is a true connection. By the power of open intelligence the spontaneity of interaction really opens up. I suppose you could say it is an extemporaneous, spontaneous quality that allows for the zenith statement to be made in whatever that interaction is. It doesn't matter what it is; it could be sitting right wherever you are or it could be talking to the toll taker on the toll road or the grocery store checker. It is such a complete, open connectivity in which everything is very direct, precise and right on. All the babbling settles in the core power of potent speech that is very directed and purposeful. This is the enormous potency of open intelligence, and it clears everything up absolutely.

All the considering we've done of our life and about how we're going to use our body, mind and speech is cleared up completely in short moments of open intelligence. The richer it is in our experience, the clearer it is to us what to do and how to act. We find within ourselves tremendous unshakable, indestructible stability that can never be taken away. With that comes the courage to act from and as that stability and to set aside all conventional outlooks, approaches and ways of looking at everything.

So, no matter what field we're in, we have a whole new panoramic vista. We can build whatever we want to build without any homage to convention whatsoever—brand new, right here. We can build that on our own or we can find other people committed to open intelligence. The easiest way to live life is with other people committed to open intelligence; it's also the most profoundly powerful. It's not the kind of situation where one has to be off and alone forever as the only one in the whole wide world who speaks open intelligence, when there are so many who are committed to it.

These choices are very powerful, and whatever they are, that's what your life is. The open intelligence choice, truly real open intelligence, is a life plan. It takes over everything and directs it without any pondering or effort at all. There simply isn't a choice any longer to go the ordinary way or to make ordinary decisions. The radical shift from being totally self-centered to being mutually aligned and mutually connected with everyone and everything is a completely different orientation, and we see that from the very beginning. In the first moment of open intelligence we're completely reoriented to our actual perception of the real world *as it is*—the open intelligence world, a world of constant solution, a world of piercing statements that connect, that go right to the heart, that bind everyone in mutuality and trust in collaboration, in power to solve any problem that might come up.

OPEN INTELLIGENCE IS THE FOREMOST EDUCATION

No matter what we do, it's important to have pride in what we do. We have the pride of open intelligence. This sort of pride isn't based on our diplomas or our résumé, all the things we've done, the family we were born into or the education and money we have. Open intelligence pride is the indestructible pride of open intelligence itself. It doesn't need any extraneous events in order to have a sense of pride. Open intelligence is pride itself; it's the core of pride without any arrogance. It is true pride, the pride that knows itself exactly *as it is*, where in each moment any thought is crystal clear.

The thoughts, emotions, sensations and experiences no longer need to have a special look or role. They just flow along, presenting themselves again and again as the rocket fuel of open intelligence. There is not even a noticing or naming them anymore; there is no need to get all wrapped up in whatever the labels are, no need to toil over philosophical questions like, "What am I supposed to be? Am I me or not me, a self or not a self?" Who cares?

Open intelligence is the foremost education. There's something in the text about that today: "The Four Mainstays of open intelligence is the foremost instruction, the education informing all others, the one that is core in every way, that comes out at the front of all other kinds of education, the one that actually has the ability to get right into our body, speech, mind, qualities and activities and unlock the power to benefit all without learning anything, an entire expanse of knowledge at our disposal."

As regards how we would build Great Freedom and Balanced View, if we had just sat around trying to learn from conventional methods, we wouldn't be sitting here today. From a few people beginning to pass the torch of open intelligence, pretty soon the whole world is lighted up and on fire. We saw the fires burning there already in over 7,600 cities on the map we looked at—all from open intelligence getting real in people's lives.

Human beings are totally precious. We always want what's best; that is always in our heart. No matter what our action is, we want what's best. Even a person who has exactly the opposite of our own data—which may seem very, very extreme to us—in their heart they want the best. It's just that we haven't had the tools to see what is the best and to see what our real power is.

Maybe we've felt so helpless and powerless that we have to look somewhere else: to a deity that lives somewhere else, to some kind of theistic structure that has control over human beings and keeps a checklist of our good points and bad points. Maybe we have felt our deity is the right one, and everybody else in the world has to follow our deity or else we're going to wipe them off the face of the earth.

It can be that way in society too if everyone gives over their totally potent energy to describing people as all kinds of different psychological or personality states, saying that each one can be categorized according to certain states or behaviors. That's one way of going about it, but we really have to ask ourselves about the results of what we're doing. Have these things brought the mental and emotional stability that they seem to hold for us, or are they a kind of dangling carrot where we think that if we do these things we'll be all right. Have they or have they not—check it out.

INFINITE POWER

Today we demand results. If we don't have a result when we click that mouse, we won't go to the Internet site again. It's the same with all the other technologies and methods that we're using to look at the way things actually are. If we try something and we don't have a direct experience of who we really are, then we're very impatient; we want to click a reset button that's really going to work. We won't tolerate any bullshit, and we're not going to fool around anymore. That's what we're demanding of ourselves right now as a human society: we demand what works.

Twenty years ago most of us had never heard of the Internet, but now we make demands that it do something for us that it isn't yet doing. Almost everyone every day has this sense, like when we click on links and they go to error pages or when the Google servers break down. Well, ten years ago most of us had nothing like that; we didn't even know how to use any of the technology that was available. We're becoming more and more demanding in our technologies, and that's why we've demanded open intelligence.

We don't want to sit around trying to figure out if we have a thought disorder or a neurotic tendency and then which one it is out of the thousands of labels that fit within that order. We don't want to enter into relationship with each other where we have to say, "I'm this neurotic tendency, these are my thought disorders, and these are your thought disorders." We're not permitting that kind of basis of relationship. We're demanding and simultaneously permitting in our own experience the total power and indestructible stability of human society—and not just of human society, but of all things.

From data our understanding of the world is extremely limited, and we can only grok our own dimension, which is the time-space continuum. However, the power of open intelligence opens up an understanding of what we are in relation to the whole world and what we are in relation to all the other dimensions of existence that from data we cannot even see. In each datum we can only see the narrow perspective of name tags and labels. From the view of open intelligence we open up to the very real, open connectivity, interactivity and interoperability of all intelligence in nature, all intelligence in all dimensions whatsoever.

Human intelligence is now massively networked. As that opens up more and more, the networking won't just be with human intelligence; it will be with all kinds of intelligences eve-rywhere. Our own intelligence will expand into a power beyond anything we can imagine, settling completely into quality, com-pletely into power, completely into the ability and the capacity to provide all resources we need.

By the power of open intelligence we open up to the natural resource that can never be depleted, and in it we find all the re-sources we need—making resources like petroleum and energy from the sun insignificant. Infinite power and memory capacity are already built in—engineered right here—and all of it is ac-cessed in this simple moment of open intelligence. This moment of open intelligence is direct accessibility and direct connectivi-ty to the potent intelligence of nature, instantiated right here.

EMPOWERING ONESELF IN OPEN INTELLIGENCE

By the power of open intelligence we move from being totally obsessed with all of our sensations, emotions, thoughts—where that is all we're thinking about—to data being totally clear with-in open intelligence. It doesn't matter whether it's occurring or not. For someone who is clear, it's easy to see whether others are really involved in their name tags or in open intelligence. Very real things come up, and they do need to be talked about in a certain way. Different people are willing to be supported at different levels.

For myself for example, when issues come up concerning my physical condition, those issues don't take over the entire pers-pective. They're a spontaneous appearance of open intelligence; they just are whatever they are. It's laughable to me; I could drop dead this instant and it would be fine with me. There's a shift that occurs from being all involved with ourselves to feel-ing expansive. Whatever our circumstantial data is, it is the ex-pressions of potent open intelligence, so we might as well get used to it!

You may have a friend who has some kind of legitimate phys-ical issue; however, it's really, really important for him to em-power himself in open intelligence as the healing force of that issue, whatever it is. Whether he gets over it and is cured or whether he dies, he will live in the ultimate cure. He will always be taking the best medicine, and your approach as a friend with him is right on: supporting him in understanding open intelligence as the entire basis shining forth from within all these medical labels. This flow of looking at things from data was set up for him early on, and so that's where he automatically goes, but it isn't a statement about who he is. It's all just his own data, and that's his learning ground and his space of experience— seeing how open intelligence shines from within all these data.

THE COMMITMENT TO OPEN INTELLIGENCE

Anyone anywhere can set up an entire work career based only on open intelligence, and you don't have to have a career where there's constant jumping from one circle into the next. "Now I have to be talking about all the data, but now I have to be talking about open intelligence." Open intelligence brings up super-integrity. "What am I doing with my life? How do I want to be living? Who do I want to be living with? Am I really willing to settle for the way it's been?" It doesn't matter how much we've accomplished in any field or what all the labels are associated with that field; we can walk away at any moment. One just says, "I won't do it the old way any longer. I will support people in open intelligence, and I will only accept patients and clients who are committed to open intelligence. That's going to be my standard of practice: continuity of care within open intelligence." It is a simple business plan, which makes it easy for you and for everyone. You make an agreement right up front to commit to open intelligence —just like a therapist makes an agreement with a patient right up front to label different diagnoses.

The commitment right at the start is the commitment to open intelligence. "This is the work we will be doing together. We will be relying on open intelligence rather than data. The context we will use for discussing all data is open intelligence, and that's what we will look to for the solutions. This isn't a setting where we will get together and talk about what's happened with the family history or this, that and the other thing. We're talking about who we are right here—opening that up, showing how that's been the basis of everything all along, no matter what we've labeled it."

The Twelve Empowerments are the great opening. They show us exactly what's going on in our life and how it's all been a great flow of open intelligence. We get to reinterpret all the misinterpretations we've had about life, all the people we've blamed and resented and all the times we've blamed and resented ourselves. We get to see all the contempt we've had for ourselves and others—all of it. It's a big relief.

It takes a lot of work to try to label all our character defects and keep them under control in the corral for shortcomings and character defects! We didn't want any of those wild animals to get out, but now we can open the gates and let all the wild animals come stomping out—even the wild animals we didn't even know we had. At first it might be a little scary, but after a while they are like dear friends. "These are my data; so what?"

We start to see that data simply undo theselves, and we don't have to do anything. Open intelligence is self-releasing in each here-and-now. There's no way to keep it in place; it slips in and out on its own. There's no way to ever capture it and analyze it and say it's made of time and space, matter and energy or anything else. How you want to spend your life within yourself and in relationship with others is entirely up to you. In a real commitment to open intelligence it becomes vividly clear how that's going to pan out.

SOLUTION-BASED SUPPORT

When I first began, I found out that there were all kinds of people who wanted to come to the training, and I found out that there were lots of people who wanted to talk about their data. At first people would call me and I would be on the phone for two hours listening to all their data streams. I thought, "Okay. Is this how I'm going to live my life?" I eventually decided that when the phone would ring, it would be a matter of, "I'll listen to your data for three minutes, then tell me what the solution is." The phone calls got much shorter! Then I decided it would be, "Don't call me anymore; email me, and in less than one paragraph tell me where it's at." No more phone calls. Then the next step was, "Well, if you want to hear what I have to say, then you have to make a 100% commitment to open intelligence." People wanted to talk about all kinds of things, so it was about deciding how I was going to spend my life.

What applies to me applies to all of us. Of course we want to be as much benefit as we can to ourselves and others, and if when we are sharing with each other we let others go on and on spewing confusion, then it isn't really helpful. We have a choice in that situation: we can either know that they're open to hearing what the solution is about that, invite them to present the solution, or just say, "Excuse me, I need to leave now." No one is ever a hostage to their own data or anyone else's.

I'm from a family where I'm the oldest of six children, and so of course I wanted everything to go right for my brothers and sisters, and I still do. However, very early on I learned that all of my ranting and raving and ideas about what they should do with their lives didn't work. Now our conversations are, "How are you? I'm glad you're doing well. I'm proud of what you've done with your life. You've been a great example to me. Let's have a nice dinner together."

No matter what our history has been with a person, we can completely change it. The kinds of relationships or conversations that are entirely overwhelmed with data alone require two people in order to have them, and the whole dynamic changes if one person doesn't buy into their data any longer. In families these dynamics can be very ingrained. "This one is supposed to be like that, this one is supposed to be like that, and that's the way it is." In open intelligence no one is supposed to be like anything.

The whole impulse to help someone in your family is really the impulse of open intelligence to live solidly in itself. However, there's no possibility of being of help to anyone—including yourself—without that open intelligence. All the cloying data that have been a habitual run of the past, such as getting into depressive states over family members or oneself, must be cut through with open intelligence. The relationship must change completely; it must be cut through at the root, with a new relationship opening up. To not continue on like it has been before is what serves you and everyone.

YOUR OWN CLEAR EXAMPLE

Every single person on earth is fully potent and capable of open intelligence, every single one, and every single person has the complete set of skillful means to support anyone else in resting in open intelligence. To say, "Oh it isn't possible for that one," is just a cop-out.

You also don't have to do any blabbing about open intelligence. Show up as the example of yourself, totally enriched with open intelligence. That's example enough, and just that has a tremendous effect on people. It starts to seep in; they look at you and say, "Wow! Look at him, he's just like me. All of a sudden I feel different." These radical changes in you have more of an effect on other people than all the talking you can do. It's a power that cuts right through all the bullshit—all the history, all the memories, all the projections of the future. Your own open intelligence is the basis of the relationship.

I talk to many people every day, and with many of them I never even mention what I do or what they ought to be doing. If someone asks, well *then*, that's a different story! The key is the request for instruction. Unless someone is requesting, there's nothing to say. "Can you give me an instruction that will benefit open intelligence?" That's a good question to ask.

It's impossible to be a true leader when the leadership is based on data alone without open intelligence. There are things that could come up like, "What will people think of me? Is this the right thing? What if this doesn't work out? Am I being too bossy?" Whatever it might be, again, open intelligence is the only solution. Your own decisive, instinctive recognition of open intelligence is inseparable from benefit, inseparable from service. Open intelligence and service are inseparable—service in open intelligence, open intelligence in service. From your own open intelligence you know what to do and how to act in each situation. If you're young, you're just getting accustomed to this; however, by the power of open intelligence it will become more and more natural to you.

As a leader, build your team so that everyone is in agreement that open intelligence is the core competence, and make sure everyone on the team receives training in open intelligence competence. If people fall out of alignment with open intelligence as the core competence, then you need to see if they still agree that they're willing to have open intelligence as the core competence. If they've decided that they are no longer willing, then they can leave the team. They've chosen to deselect themselves, because the team's agreement is the core competence of open intelligence.

THE SIGN, EVIDENCE AND DEMONSTRATION OF OPEN INTELLIGENCE

We're trained to think that when we have an afflictive state it's ours. "It's all mine, my hideous little world." But by the power of open intelligence, we begin to see that this afflictive state represents the same afflictive state of multitudinous beings. The realms of health, sexuality, worries about money are all a direct reflection and mirror-like responsiveness to the afflictive states of countless beings. It is all the dynamic energy of total potency, of total power and freedom.

Be present to those afflictive states in their arising. Shining forth from within them is total power, total indestructibility, total and complete sovereignty. There is nothing to be afraid of in oneself or others. Power comes from allowing everything to be *as it is*. At first there is an understanding: "Wow, nothing has an independent nature!" Just the simple intellectual understanding alone is such a boon; it is such an incredible good fortune.

By the power of introduction to open intelligence in short moments, that intellectual understanding slips naturally into instinctive recognition. That instinctive recognition and understanding are the first evidence and demonstration of potent benefit; there is no destination of benefit to get to, no destination of service to get to. Open intelligence itself, potent benefit to every one of us immediately, no matter what our afflictive state is, is the sign, evidence and demonstration of the potency of open intelligence.

The fear of one's own self slips away in the instinctive recognition. It is the fearlessness of instinctive recognition—being able to encounter everything, no matter how hideous. All the gruesome, heinous metaphors popping up relating to one's experience of oneself—hells and heavens and everything in between—are all the potency of open intelligence. Any one of them can become a whole world if we want to go in there. The simplicity and solidity carry us through. Everything all at once—understanding, instinctive recognition, potent benefit—is in each moment inseparable.

If your own data seems unbearable, rely on the Four Mainstays. Rugged, rugged! If you're the last person on earth, the Four Mainstays are rugged. Stay with what you are, always in your indestructible nature. You can't get out of it; you might as well acknowledge it! All the special flavors of your individualized identity, whatever they are, they're expressions of the indivisible identity that unites us all in great mutuality.

As a society we're looking for release from all our problems by coming up with intellectual solutions; however, the solution is in getting real with who we are. That's where our potency is. It doesn't mean sitting around and talking about it. It means recognizing in the instant of our afflictive states the potency that prevails. This is very humbling after all the efforting, paper shuffling and gigabytes of information. Very humbling.

In the kind of humility that we find within ourselves, we find what is really stable. Everything we've tried to avoid—the deep dark feelings that we have, the emotions, the thoughts, the memories we don't want to think about, the sensations we don't want to encounter, accidents, aging, sickness death—in all of this open intelligence is sovereign, and all of it is a demonstration of the potency of open intelligence.

All afflictive states whatsoever are the evidence of indestructibility. We learn that they will destroy us, and they can if we think they're real. We sometimes may tend to get spaced out, but in afflictive states we're not spaced out at all. We're solid to the core, right? We know where the energy is.

It's not in some weird realm over there where blissful beings are hanging out. The afflictive states *are* the blissful beings, interestingly enough. This is what open intelligence allows us: the good fortune, the incredible gift, the most wonderful boon of release and relief from all the psychological and intellectual turmoil and struggle. By the power of open intelligence we see solutions to what ails us.

OPEN INTELLIGENCE GUIDES THE WAY

Never too young, never too old—if you're just at the beginning with a simple understanding, or if you have broken through all afflictive states whatsoever, it matters not. You're in the indestructible open intelligence family. No one can ever get out of it—no one is born into it, no one dies outside of it. Open intelligence is the constant affiliation throughout all circumstances, where one is always loved, provided for and taken care of.

No matter what the age or the circumstance is, open intelligence is the pervasive core of any kind of educational process. So, any situation that you are in that you hope to learn about and that you hope to be able to contribute something to, the answer is in open intelligence. The commitment first is to open intelligence, and the instruction is from there. How do we gain confidence in open intelligence to the point of complete surety? It's by trusting it moment-to-moment. Then it's the absolute priority.

Then open intelligence guides the way and not all the muttering! Open intelligence shows what to do and how to act. The demand to be a certain way, to perform a certain way, to do things a certain way in order to have what we need—all of that settles down. More and more all is given in mutual responsiveness, everyone taking care of each other naturally without any elaborate systems of bartering or exchange. I see this totally alive in the great courage of allowing everything to be *as it is*—the dynamic energy of open intelligence. No need to indulge data, avoid it or replace it, nothing to hide out from, no one to hide out.

Maybe you have heard some things here that you have never even knew you felt, but when you heard it from someone else, it felt like you were being ripped to shreds. That's because that's *you*, too. That's why it strikes you so deeply from out of the blue. All of this is within us. It is a greatly empowering situation for everyone to share everything *as it is* without getting into a big story about it. In this simple way everything is known to be like pure space, and all of us instinctively recognize this in exactly the same way. It's in the pit of hell—realizing that pleasant states are no different from extremely afflictive ones.

In my own case, all of a sudden all of these afflictive states grabbed me by the throat and throttled me to the ground, and there weren't any antidotes that worked anymore. That's the same as it is for everyone listening to or reading these talks, or you wouldn't be listening and reading; the antidotes don't work anymore. The open intelligence solution is the key, and just like you, this is what I saw. So, we are evidence of that to each other: short moments, inseparable from the energy of the afflictive state.

If we let the afflictive state be *as it is*—boom! Instead of being all wiped out or depressed by everything that we're feeling, we feel energized, fearless, fierce and wrathful. Some of us have more experience in knowing what our afflictive states are. We've been around for decades examining our afflictive states, and maybe we've had friends with whom we could talk about our afflictive states for hours and hours. "Oh, you wouldn't believe my mother and father, my school teachers, the church and everything else," or whatever our complaint is.

By letting everything be *as it is*, we open up into this whole new arena of the real depth and profundity of what it is to be a human being. We really get it; we totally and completely get that we are helplessly attracted in open intelligence. We are completely together in the potent force of open intelligence. Connect in: that's what short moments is. We all want connection, and that's where connection is—it's in that short moment.

Value Letters from Participants

There are certain afflictive data that I have encountered throughout my life, and worries about money would be one of the foremost. Cares about money have ruled my family, and there has been the feeling that lack of money was the cause of suffering for the family.

The other day I received a mail from back home, and I was reminded that, indeed, there still is a world out there that has not left suffering behind. My mum was writing to say that she was distressed over her circumstances—about money, her career and the utter futility of life. I began to type out all my ideas about how to make it better, but then I just stopped and deleted it all. Rather than write out something based on data—whether hers or mine—I simply expressed my sincere gratitude for her and everything in my life, and that was it. I felt incredibly heartbroken by the suffering, but guided by instinctive open intelligence in the same instant.

As I become more comfortable with this natural abundance of open intelligence, I can see that I can be supportive for my family. I can stand strong in all the afflictions and assure myself and others around me of abundance, no matter how many labels come up.

I find that no matter what the amount of money I have had, the same sorts of data come up. "I have too much. I have too little. I am too stingy. I spend too much"—a dizzying display when taken to have a nature separate from the complete driving force of open intelligence.

Data about my career meander back and forth: about how I am going to obtain notoriety, how I am going to make something of myself and how I am going to be the best of the best in whatever I am doing. These can be incredibly afflictive. I see through the eyes of open intelligence that wanting to be the best of the best is the natural drive of wanting to be of profound benefit, that's all. There's no need to get lost down differing rabbit holes and get nowhere; I just harness this power to make steady, clear actions that support me in gaining confidence in open intelligence.

Throughout my life I have found comfort in withdrawing myself from social circumstances. Often I have felt there was a sort of judge commenting on every word I said, and so I chose to not speak or relate with people. I still prefer not to speak often, but the view I have of myself being an awkward, socially retarded person is nothing that hinders me anymore. It's still so common that these data come up when relating, and in a busy community circumstance such as this I could say constant social affliction is very pervasive, but these feelings no longer dictate my actions. I am forever grateful for this new relationship with my afflictive states.

There is no need to see these data as anything other than powerful indications of my true clear nature.

SECOND SHARE

I have given up trying to write the perfect value letter with the perfect answers! In the text today I read, "Each here-and-now *as it is*, is the gift of open intelligence." These are great words that resonate deeply—instructions that I know I need to investigate more profoundly in my own everyday experience.

It is stated clearly that the beneficial powers that open intelligence offers increase as we recognize the obviousness of open intelligence. So, if I don't see much of these beneficial powers expressed in my life, it is simply an invitation to rely more on the Four Mainstays and strengthen my commitment to open intelligence. There is no need to dwell on the lack of progress; just hold the head up high and rely on open intelligence again and again. In the midst of comparison, self-blame and doubt, open intelligence shines powerfully. This I am starting to see. Hearing the proof from other participants and teachers makes the trust that it is possible grow stronger, even for me.

Thank you for the opportunity to name and share my most afflictive data. Here they come! One of my favorites that keeps coming up in different shapes is, "I am wrong, flawed, a loser." It is self-doubt in different forms and also fear of doing wrong and hurting others. This is how the storyline can go: "I have wasted my life by making wrong decisions. Everyone is doing so much better. Everyone can implement the one simple change but me. I am faking it. I don't seem to make anything worthy out of this life. I am a victim of wrong decisions. I should have been an actress, a dancer, a singer, an environmental activist or some other prominent figure. I have destroyed my child by making wrong decisions. I am responsible for my family's suffering. I am too selfish. There is no hope." A sadness that feels unending and deep as the deepest ocean can often follow these viewpoints.

Here are some other favorites that can really grip me: the idea that one day it will all be fine when I am really stable in relying on open intelligence, when I find the perfect job, when I am retired, when I die. There is the longing for the perfect partner, the prince who is going to save me, and fear that he will never show up. There is the need for others' confirmation and love in order to feel good about myself; sexual desire; I am better and different from everybody else; wanting my family and especially my son to behave in a certain ways; money—that I have to make it, that I am not responsible with it; food-indulgence.

Some of the viewpoints of fear of making wrong decisions in regards to my child have been coming up. I gently allowed them to be, and I take short moments when the endless story-making starts up. There is a subtle notion that these afflictive data can be experienced as pure beneficial power and open intelligence when I just allow them to flow on by. The trust is growing that they cannot hurt me, that there is nothing to fear.

I find it very helpful to listen to downloads and turn to my trainer when I feel unable to rest with afflictive data. I borrow trust from trainers and friends who have resolved their own afflictive data.

It makes me smile writing these down. Just like black letters on the computer leave no trace on the computer itself, they leave no trace anywhere. They can all be deleted in a moment of open intelligence.

Day Six

DEATH AND OTHER AFFLICTIVE DATA

The Written Text

When the utter lucidity of death is initially obvious, it is important not to stray from lucid open intelligence and to simply relax and allow it to be *as it is*—a blissful expanse free of misery.

The indestructible Four Mainstays—open intelligence, trainer, training and community—carry over seamlessly into death as a blissful expanse, without separation. You are completely at ease and cared for, without even the need for a body, breathing or communication. The signs of death appear as increase and evidence of the potency of open intelligence. This is easy if you have been introduced to open intelligence and practiced even slightly.

Immediately upon death there is the absolute resolution of all data in primordial bliss—bright and aware. All attachment and clinging go forever. Past data are clear and open without a trace. Present data are clear and open without a trace. Future data are clear and open without a trace. This is the tremendous release into blissful brightness and joy. By knowing right now exactly what death is—the powerful blissfulness and joy of totally open intelligence—everyone is prepared for death.

Always expect death to come at any time. Simply carry on remaining composed as open intelligence. This is the proper attitude. If strong panic and fearful images appear during life or death, utter lucidity immediately devours them as its own blissful energy.

By the power of the assurance of open intelligence in all data, death comes easily, knowing that all images arise as in a hologram or rainbow, vanishing naturally without a trace. So right now, rest assuredly in open intelligence as afflictive states appear. The open intelligence you rest in is shining forth within the afflictive state and is not looking at it from a distance, like a cat watching a mouse. At the moment of death there is no going from one place to another. There is simply a super-complete and blissful bright state, which is free from someone going somewhere.

When dying, do not worry about what will happen to your possessions—including your body. Let whoever wants them take them, like something without an owner. Simply rest blissfully, as primordial open intelligence. There will be a buoyant and light feeling, like space pouring into space or sunlight in air. Since nothing appears that is not free in your own place of utterly lucid open intelligence, rest vividly without thinking of anything whatsoever.

When the breathing body stops, the great luminosity arises, like a clear sky dawning—your own nature. You rest as this continuity of perfection. Therefore, it is best to be weary of identification with data and decide you have had enough. Thus, come to terms right now with the importance of recognizing that disturbing emotions are simply the names of the tremendous power of open intelligence.

Relax in the power of open intelligence and carry on realizing the power and meaning of data being free of limiting influence. Data arise, endure and subside naturally like an invisible breeze in space. With authentic reliance on the power of open intelligence, disturbing states are undermined.

The principle of the beneficial power of open intelligence is in its surge of data. Carry on instinctively, recognizing ordinary open intelligence as the surge of each here-and-now. It is impossible for open intelligence to become undermined by data, so just relax like the powerful ease of the great ocean, filled with vital energy and power regardless of ups and downs.

With open intelligence as the single focus, no countermeasure or curative fantasy is necessary to effect relief, and so antidotes to disturbing states are done away with. Because "you" are the surge of open intelligence itself, excessive interest in data is subsumed in very vivid open intelligence, and their stories and patterns reside in their innate beneficial power and energy.

Because the simple lucidity of open intelligence undermines the very idea of the existence of non-recognition of open intelligence, non-recognition is thoroughly cut at the root. Because sensory impressions and visual images are fueled only by open intelligence, by sustaining its essence they are recognized to be the power of open intelligence.

Similarly, sounds of all kinds—evident due to open intelligence—are all recognized equally as self-sounds of open intelligence and are like an echo unfolding in air—pure, clear and without effect. Thus sensory impressions, visual images and sounds are the powerful dynamic energy of open intelligence.

Due to this there are no compelling stories or emotional reactions whatsoever, and the disturbing aspect of data is exhausted completely. There is complete power shining from within all descriptive frameworks. Data are the surging beneficial power of open intelligence itself, and this is the crucial point.

By the power of open intelligence, all subtle data are settled into a natural state of indestructible stability, so it does not need to be forced to enter into a stable state by applying counter measures designed to oppose them as some kind of danger or threat. When all data are left to flow on by, they ramp up to their natural potency. Everything is perceived as the power of open intelligence rather than as manifestations of confusion, disturbance, affliction or reification.

Open intelligence is the supercharged beneficial power devouring data. Open intelligence demonstrates power in its actual expression as immediate circumstances. This is complete power in all experience, complete perceptual openness in all experience, freedom in immediate perception.

The power of directly encountering all disturbing mental, emotional, physical and experiential states as the actual potent force of beneficial power allows you to plan for death without shrinking away from it. Simply said: injury, sickness, aging and death are another series of emphatic statements of the actual potent force of open intelligence's all-consuming, indestructible power. By the power of open intelligence, all data are raw and real power of open intelligence. The intensity of allowing all data to be as they are breaks through to obvious open intelligence at all times.

Letting all data be as they actually are, there is a supercharged expanse of intelligent benefit, superpower and surety, the emptying of all data of their ignorant meaning forever, and the great launching of universal benefit, potency and accord.

The Four Mainstays are the indestructible vehicle comprised of the open intelligence body, speech, mind, qualities and activities, living boldly and freely, aware that death can come at any moment, completely prepared and relaxed about it—open intelligence the only relation, purpose and meaning in all data. Right now, without hesitation, carry on extracting and totally enjoying the power of all data.

Day Six Talk

Anyone here who wants to live a life in open intelligence community can do so; it's a matter of making a commitment to it. Just like the commitment is made to 100% open intelligence, so we see within ourselves that we are capable; we actually have the power to design our life to be as we want it to be. If we want to hang out with other people committed to open intelligence, we can hang out with them; if we want to work only with people committed to open intelligence, we can do that. In open intelligence itself the power and courage to make changes we never dreamt of comes about.

In Balanced View we have a whole training on team building according to open intelligence—very specific trainings on how to build an organization based on it. We are working with teams of people in all kinds of settings: in neuroscience, the scholarship of religion, and alcohol and drug treatment, just to name a few. In these different settings the people working on that particular project work in open intelligence teams.

The power of open intelligence is such that it clarifies all the elaborations and descriptions we've been using to describe everything. It clarifies their true meaning and at the same time sheds precise light on whatever the description is. By the power of open intelligence we tap into the essential fundamental nature of all descriptions; thus we are able to have very vivid insight into the nature of all descriptions.

There is no way for human society to advance in a way that is completely beneficial unless we ramp up our intelligence into open intelligence; that's all there is to it. Open intelligence has the answers we're looking for. No matter what our field or profession is, open intelligence has the answer to that profession. It just requires one person in that particular profession who is totally committed to open intelligence to build a team related to that profession and to innovate it completely.

This is exactly what has happened right here at the Center in Skåne, so we have a solid example that it works. All kinds of mixed up ideas and vagueness and misunderstandings are completely cleared up due to the empowerment of a team of people.

What is required anywhere else is similar to what is required right here.

INCREDIBLY POWERFUL SKILLFUL MEANS

There are incredible powerful skillful means for actually consistently fulfilling the power of beneficial and creative intent. That only comes from open intelligence. It can only come from people whose minds and bodies are saturated in the vital liveliness of open intelligence; it can't come from people thinking about data, no matter how sophisticated the data are. Without adding in this fundamental piece to all the things everyone is thinking about in such an advanced way, there can be no real breakthroughs to where people want to go. The breakthroughs that do occur will be limited because they will have an incorrect understanding of the nature of the way things actually are. So, again, this is absolutely key.

All it takes is you making the commitment in one area and then building a powerful team based on the core competence of open intelligence. That means that when you advertise the job description and people show up to take the job, everyone involved is required to have the core commitment to open intelligence. It will be understood from the beginning that if they decided to go off and get involved in a bunch of data, then they have made a choice to leave the team and to deselect themselves. There is no one to fire them; they fire themselves. This is very easy to manage and put into practice. If someone goes off into a rage of data, you just meet with the person and say, "Here's the agreement you signed. You signed this agreement to 100% open intelligence teaming. Are you still aligned to this agreement?" They will either say yes or no. It is so easy.

Open intelligence breeds open intelligence, just like you can see here at the Center: everyone being together, able to do things that would seem impossible, like purchase this Center one day and have a completely full retreat the next day. It was November three years ago when we first hit the ground running, jumping in fully—body, speech, mind, qualities and activities. As the laser-like brightness of open intelligence outshines meaningless elaborations, then everything about the elaborations

110

that might work in some way to carry out a task becomes very clear. The tool set is there, but it is never any final law in its own right.

COMPLETELY DIFFERENT WAYS OF FINDING SOLUTIONS

Say, for example, due to our elaborations we believe that we are limited to a continuum based on time-space and causality, and we have 100% committed to the belief in the time-space continuum. The only solutions we can see to problems are in the time-space causality continuum. It makes perfect sense; the reasoning behind the assumptions is simple, anyone can get it, and it's based on fundamental logic. However, there is a more comprehensive order that subsumes the current order we believe to exist. By discovering that, we discover something fundamental, not only to the time-space continuum, but also to all dimensions and continuums of reality.

That discovery opens up into activity and interoperability with all other dimensions. We're no long limited to a communication network that is just based on the laws of the time-space continuum, mass and energy in order to provide computing power and memory storage. We're no longer limited to matter and energy. Those are tools of time, space and dimensionality—the way we currently understand it—which are built through causal means.

However, from the piercing view of open intelligence we're able to see completely different ways of approaching problems and completely different ways of opening up our communication processes. For example, by recognizing open intelligence and data we start to loosen up. We don't see ourselves in such a fixed, defined way anymore as only a single identity, where we're locked into an individualized identity forever.

The vantage of open intelligence and data allows us to liken ourselves more to something like the Internet, which is an overall view containing all kinds of information processes, which are analogous to a stream of data, you could say. Thus, we can see ourselves simply as an information process within the great singularity. All of these are synonymous: the singularity, open intelligence, the view—synonymous; points of view/data and information processes—synonymous.

These are very simple ways of getting down to the basics of physical reality without going off into an extreme tangent. Most importantly it is required that you know this instinctively in your own experience in order to incorporate it into any kind of knowledge system. If you're an engineer or a philosopher or whatever you are, then the only way to make an advance in your field that is all beneficial and has never been made before is by the power of open intelligence. Only there can you lighten up enough to say, "I don't care what anyone thinks. I know this for sure from my own experience, and I am going to start to advance based on what I know."

For example, there are all kinds of ways the technology underlying Great Freedom and Balanced View could be presented; however, by the view of open intelligence it's possible to see how humans really work. We're not really so complicated as we are told we are. We're not governed by all of the laws of time-space causality that we learned we are governed by. We've learned all kinds of things about ourselves: that we're fixed entities and that the only way to heal our bodies exists within fiddling around with things within the time-space causality continuum—through pharmaceuticals, surgeries, chemotherapy, whatever all these things are. We have learned to maintain our physical health through all kinds of physical processes—data about the way to get us balanced. But that has happened so rarely in a totally conclusive way for anyone, so why keep doing it?

We're result–oriented; we want things that work. We don't want to keep doing the same thing over and over again that hasn't worked, expecting a different result. That doesn't make any sense. Would you do the same thing over and over again that didn't work? No! If it doesn't work, it doesn't work, but if it *does* work, you can build on it.

CUTTING THROUGH ALL LIMITING ELABORATIONS

I've talked a little bit about physical health, but now let's look at mental health. We have gotten so lost and confused in this particular area, and without open intelligence it's impossible to have an overview of how true mental health can possibly come about. Only with open intelligence is it possible to see the basic bio-engineering principals behind how we identify ourselves as being this way or that. Then once that is seen, it's possible to clearly name those things as "open intelligence" and "data." It's as simple as that, so why go on talking to yourself or anyone else in any other way? It's an elective process, and you are never a hostage or victim to all the elaborations.

They are all fueled by open intelligence and are the surge of its beneficial power. Any elaboration is the surge of its beneficial power. Your body is the surge of its beneficial power; your speech is the surge of its power; your mind is the surge of its beneficial power, and your qualities and activities are the surge of the beneficial power of open intelligence. By the power of short moments, it becomes incredibly obvious that the power of your body, speech, mind, qualities and activities is diminished, demeaned and boxed in by continuing to label yourself according to definitions other than open intelligence and by continuing to box yourself in to a personality type or a diagnosis of some kind. There is no need to sit around and talk in a meek and disempowered way.

Say you were totally involved in religion or psychology, and now you have a strong taste of open intelligence and it is very real for you. You can begin to see, hmm, this religion I believed in or this practice of psychology looks a lot different if looked at from the vantage of open intelligence rather than from the vantage of the data alone.

The data stream of being afraid of what comes next can be a little scary, but it is just another surge of the power of open intelligence opening up a new way of looking at things. What is most important is to be comfortable and assured in your own experience. The descriptive frameworks cannot help you; only the surety and power found in your own experience can help you. So, this is absolutely key.

We as a human society right now are in the very process of sharply releasing and cutting through at the root all the limiting elaborations that we've been applying to ourselves. We've never been able to make any kind of breakthrough that would assure mental and emotional stability in the millions of years of human society, but now we have. That is the power of open intelligence right there. Is open intelligence yet another complicated solution that no one can understand unless they've gone to school for about twenty years and even then they don't really understand it and can't even apply it in their own life? No, it isn't like that at all. It's something simple and direct, but at the same time it plays out with brilliant complexity. It brings us into an optimal state of functioning that completely devours all of our elaborations as its own energy and fuel.

We have this profound capacity within ourselves to bring forth technologies that are extraordinarily beneficial, that make all of our current models obsolete, just like this makes models of dealing with mental stability obsolete. It's a core education that needs to be trained into human society from the beginning of life. That's just the way it is; it completely turns over all our ideas about everything.

CONCERNS ABOUT MONEY

People here at the retreat keep bringing up money in their questions and comments. For example, "Of course food and shelter come from money. I know they do!" However, this is a perception we have been trained in, and the only way to subsume it is in your own experience. If you continue to believe that money is provisioning everything, then it's going to be impossible to get to the core.

Open intelligence is all-powerful and is at the root of the provisioning of everything. All of the money ever possessed—past, present and future—is within open intelligence. So, if you want some of it, open intelligence is the place to look for it, not in the money itself.

Open intelligence is surety. Have you ever hung out in a place that isn't good for you? You just know something bad is going to happen there, but you do it anyway. It's the same way with some of these data sets. If you hang out there, you know something's going to happen to you that you won't like or that you might regret later. Money might be one of these data sets for you.

You don't have to be in any hurry; there's no need to come to an absolute conclusion about this right here today—immediately—although you're completely free to do so if you'd like to. However, by the direct encounter with this data set in your own experience, if you don't already, you will grow to see it as the surge of total prosperity, as the surge of fulfilling an unimaginable scope of ability to consistently produce whatever you need or want.

Value Letters from Participants

I had all of what conventional life could offer: nice parents, beautiful sisters, a peaceful childhood on a small farm in one of the richest countries in the world, a good education, a loving husband, a beautiful home, a great career, money and perfect health. I could say that I had it all. In a perfect world there was nowhere for an existential depression to penetrate, but it did, because there are no conventional comforts that are waterproof in the rain of data.

In my early thirties it all started to fall apart, one thing after the other. One day there was no husband or great career anymore. My mastery in creating comfortable circumstances did not work any longer and neither did my strategies of controlling my inner and outer circumstances. There was no more energy to please everyone. My passion for changing the world disappeared into cynicism and sadness. I was left with heartbreak over a failed marriage and other failed intimate relationships I attempted to have. This was mixed with raging fear that I would never meet Mr. Right before it was too late to have children. There was nothing to hold on to anymore.

I tried to continue to work, but soon I collapsed into a two-year depression, and wherever I turned I couldn't find any meaning in life. The support I got just gave me more negative ideas about people, places and things that I could blame for my circumstances. I searched high and low for contentment and stability in my life. I tried conventional psychotherapy; I became a spiritual seeker shopping around in the world of alternative therapies and workshops, but at best I could only find temporary relief.

Spinning around in loneliness, total despair, panic and overwhelming sadness I could not see how this would ever change. I indulged in these afflictions day in and day out. The thought of this being an endless afflicted state that would go on forever made me think that maybe suicide was best, but I was too scared to do it. My self-confidence was below zero. Even to pay bills or to answer the telephone seemed too big of a task. The great success I had had in my career felt like a distant dream, as if it had never happened.

Now I could not even work. I was full of guilt and self-blame towards my husband. I ate unhealthy food and gained weight, ate even more food to punish myself and started to hate myself even more. I had a constant chatter in my head telling what I failure I was.

I took the Empowerments Training here at the Center exactly two years ago. The transition for me was immediate. After the training I went straight back to my job and told my boss and my doctor that I was okay again and that I could work 100% again. And so I did, with no problem. For me it was a matter of being able to see my victim story from the vantage of open intelligence. When no attention was given to Ms Victim, she soon disappeared.

After four months I left my job, but this time it was because I clearly saw that the job did not serve my best potential as a human being. That was a good decision, because now I am here! I now have less money and conventional career status, but there is a deep and all-pervasive knowing that I am so much more than what I own or what people say about me or what I say about myself. So, so much more.

I can still have data of loneliness, deep sadness and that life has no meaning, but when I don't indulge in them, they just eventually float away. I do not take them to be anything special; they are just my simple human experience. That is so totally humbling, but at the same time so, so powerful.

The courage to face my so-called monsters with unwavering open intelligence has showed me that I can be clear and stable in the stormiest ocean of afflictions. Wow! That leaves me with endless gratitude for the ultimate human potential that becomes evident when data are left as they are. It leaves me with the great yearning to be of benefit, benefit, benefit.

In gratitude to my afflicted states and my courage and willingness to see them just as they are.

A few years ago I had a view of the world that saw society as an incredible failure; I saw a mess and struggled to either be a part of it or be apart from it. I saw the world as being always in opposition to me, and I dreamt it would someday be something I could release myself from. Then there were times when the world was good to me, and I felt elated and wanted to go along for the ride.

Man of Constant Sorrow by Bob Dylan was a song I listened to very frequently; the lyrics confirmed for me that, yes, life is a struggle, and this is just what we have to do, so deal with it. There was also the great cultural icon of the "Aussie battler," with a whole nation affirming that it is noble to struggle and being proud, that this is what we do best.

The first time I did the Peace Training I was overwhelmed by the confidence and surety that the text and trainers were conveying. They said harmony and world peace in human society are possible and explained *how* they are possible. I had heard bold statements like that before, but never had I heard them backed up with clear and precise instructions, endless support and complete dedication for this to come about. When I actually sit and comprehend the enormity of the words "for the benefit of all," I am in complete awe of this ultimate goal. I would have classed it as outlandish and impossible some years ago, now it is obvious, simple and inevitable.

Last night, out of curiosity I listened for the first time in over a year to *Man of Constant Sorrow*, and the lines struck the same old familiar chords, but it was no longer possible for me to find any identity in those lyrics or the feelings they evoked. The man of constant sorrow seemed now far off in the distance, like an old friend waving from a faraway ship that had set sail. And so, as I find I can enjoy the unique drones and mumbles of Mr. Dylan more freely, so too I find I can let all my own unique mumbles rest freely as they are. Constant sorrow is constant energy—clear and simple, radically beneficial.

I am so honored and excited to be here sharing this adventure with you all, sharing a complete commitment to the benefit of all. After spending a few weeks here at the Center, I am incredibly inspired by so many clear and resilient individuals. You all leave me completely convinced that this open intelligence will exponentially increase. It will continue spreading and growing with the same ease as these Swedish grass fields.

Day Seven

THE BLAST THAT BLOWS OPEN
THE HERE-AND-NOW

The Written Text

A forceful blast of introduction to open intelligence blows everything wide open. These are three inseparable power-points:

1. Introduce open intelligence.
2. Rely on open intelligence.
3. Display the immediate open intelligence power.

Living like this, each here-and-now presents no difficulty and releases itself. The power-charge of the Four Mainstays accelerates the recognition and force of open intelligence in your own experience.

The authority of the introduction to open intelligence blows wide open the vast open intelligence view, so that limiting descriptions do not take hold. First, stop thinking. A bare openness remains. Not thinking, remain without thought. In that naked view is an even registering of everything that appears in the here-and-now. Next, descriptions begin to arise and are due to bare clarity openness. The descriptions are the surge of the power of open intelligence to exalt you and human society with beneficial qualities and activities—open intelligence in all experience, complete freedom in immediate perception.

The naked open intelligence view's power is trained up to potent luminosity by instinctively recognizing that all data are simply the super-surge of open intelligence, regardless of description. Open intelligence and data are inseparable like the sky and the color blue. Data that shine forth in open intelligence are the dynamic power of open intelligence itself, like very powerful light at high noon filling the sky. The training up of open intelligence is similar to the light of dawn developing into the full light of high noon. Upon initial introduction, open intelligence is obvious right away; over time it grows brighter and brighter, simple as that.

The force of this introduction delivers the sudden, sharp blasting open of all data—a thorough blow. "Thorough blow" means data are blown open fully, completely in indivisible, instinctive open intelligence. The seeming solidity, power and influence of reification—granting data an independent nature—is blown open so as to get to the obvious reality that is always present.

"Thorough blow" is explained with the example of blowing open an atomic particle. An atomic particle cannot be blown open with a weak force such that the power isn't strong enough or quite complete, and subatomic particles remain. Alternatively, the atomic particle could be blown up—forced open—with one decisive force, such that the atomic particle is completely and definitely opened into super-pure, seamless energy and power with no particle remaining—an entirely new but always present and pervasive basic reality.

That kind of thorough blow is what is meant here; one that is doubtless and unquestionably so. The term "thorough blow" means data are decisively blown open, regardless of their description, so as to arrive directly at their all-pervasive open intelligence power.

An infinitely increasing surge of open intelligence is spontaneously present, the binding force of all viewpoints. Each here-and-now is ripe with all-potent dynamic open intelligence, an infinitely increasing surge of expansive intelligence, prosperity and generosity. Dynamic benefit, a super-pure, seamless energy and power are always already present.

Introduction to open intelligence—our super-identity—is a thorough blow, unleashing open ended power right now in everyday experience. Data vanish into their basis, and the powerful expanse which pervades them is vivid. This is the introduction to the unending open intelligence power.

Day Seven Talk

EDUCATING OUR CHILDREN

Some children have a natural disposition to open intelligence, so it's very important for human society to give all the support it can to those children who have that disposition. If children do not have a natural disposition, it's important to still encourage them—especially through one's own example—to rely on open intelligence. Then if they still choose to not rely on it, we can show them how to cultivate positive data. These are the two approaches with children: either relying on open intelligence or cultivating positive data.

In an open relationship of total respect and trust, the respect and trust come from knowing for sure that each individual has the capacity to rely on open intelligence. There isn't anyone anywhere who does not have the capacity to rely on open intelligence. Everyone can be introduced to open intelligence, and then it's up to them to rely on it, but if they will not rely on it, then it is paramount to cultivate positive states in order to be happy within themselves and in good relationship with other people. However, open intelligence makes it easy, because then the natural relating with everyone and everything is open and pervasive. This is clear from the beginning, in the first moment of introduction. It blasts open everything; it blasts open all the data that seem so locked in place, and then we simply get used to it.

Basically we treat children like they have no capabilities and that they need to learn them all from us. It's very important to be firmly assured within oneself that everyone is fully endowed with open intelligence, no matter what their expression may be that seems otherwise. I am absolutely convinced that this is what has given me the relationship I have with my own children. The relationship is endowed with my absolute assurance that they are fully capable, and so everything that goes on with us is based on that fundamental premise. Very simple. I've always felt that way about them, so it's been easy. I know that within themselves they have the power to make good choices and decisions.

In open intelligence we know how to educate our children. We don't have to put our children into places that train them to be their data. Today it's easy to have an educational process for any child that is really top notch, and it will be increasingly that way. Children won't need to go to a special place called "school" anymore; a lot of the schooling will take place right at home or in another location. All of the education would be extremely high quality, with everyone in the world having equal access to the finest education. It's happening right now, and it will continue to happen and will sharply accelerate.

It's a very simple matter to provide a fantastic education to everyone on earth through very simple technologies that we have available today. A single individual has committed himself to providing the finest math education available through the Khan Academy, which considers every single angle on mathematics—from basic mathematics to the most advanced mathematics related to economics and how to apply all of it in everyday life. That's already available to everyone, and there are many other similar educational offerings. What an exciting turning point, and to package that together with open intelligence—wow! We are something else! I'm so excited that I live at this time.

THE GREATEST HEALING METHOD

We can't get out of seeing the innate mental and emotional stability we all carry. There's no way we can escape from that. It's out now; it has come out of the closet! People will naturally stop talking about themselves as a pathological condition and as someone who is weighed down by all kinds of ideas. We're not talking about going from one place to another; we're talking about this *right here*. We're demanding it of ourselves, like with all other evolutionary leaps.

We have trained ourselves to see our own identity as a complexity of all these descriptions, and then because we treated ourselves that way, when we looked at others, that was all we saw. We thought that they were only their descriptions. When we no longer see ourselves as our descriptions, then when we look out there and, wow, everyone looks great—so capable and so complete. Even if a person is acting in a totally bizarre fashion, there's still complete assurance that the person has everything they need to have complete mental and emotional stability.

Some of the people we meet may have radical mental and emotional instability, but to meet that person with the complete assurance and confidence that their mental and emotional stability is innate is the greatest healing method that anyone can ever possibly bring to another person. That occurs without having to say anything. Whether it's with children or with someone in an extreme state, this is a very powerful way of touching another human being—again, without ever saying anything. For me no one is their data stream—it's absolutely impossible—and that confidence only comes from one's knowledge of oneself and complete open intelligence about the way things actually are.

PERSIST IN OPEN INTELLIGENCE

It is important to realize that the strategy of cultivating positive states is a last ditch resort. So, that will clear that up right away! There are a lot of schemes about producing what we think we need: a healthy business, financial capability, the right kind of relationship interaction; however, in open intelligence there is no scheme whatsoever. The prime directive of open intelligence is fueled by itself, and out of that comes the activity. There are no predesigned activities; every interaction is spontaneous.

In open intelligence we're able to greet life with a tremendous force and ferocity of absolutely appropriate connection that is a truly real love—a love that allows for a full range of true love-relating rather than whatever choked ideas we have had about being with each other. There isn't anything we need to figure out about ourselves. All we need to do is rely on open intelligence.

If we want to know about our femininity or our masculinity, it's already done in open intelligence. By the power of open intelligence we are a real person, a real identity without any fakery, without a bunch of trumped-up ideas about who we are, who we've been and who we'll be in the future. We have learned to make everything so complicated, but we find out that it's actually very simple—but at the same time very radical, very fruitful, very fired up, very juiced up right now. This is the easy way.

Cultivating positive states is simply something that people do—until they are introduced to open intelligence. After that, cultivating positive states is no longer an option. Positive states, neutral states and negative states are an expanse of equalness. If we're trying to cultivate any particular state, then it doesn't allow for the power of open intelligence to show up.

The kinds of power and profound and potent insights that are in open intelligence are completely inaccessible when one is cultivating positive states. You could try to cultivate the most refined intellect ever known to humankind in relation to any subject, and it would have no potency compared to coupling that same knowledge with open intelligence. It would just be so far beyond anything that one could ever have gotten out of merely cultivating positive states. Persist in open intelligence assurance, open intelligence familiarization and open intelligence confidence; persist in that alone and you'll know exactly how to proceed.

TRUE HEALING

If you are in a healing profession, it's really important to first of all gain confidence in open intelligence in relation to all of your own data before ever advising others about anything. Unless we get beyond the current cause-and-effect intelligence that we're playing out all the time, we will never really know how powerful we are in relation to circumstances. By dealing with the issue only from data, the best that can be presented to a person is a range of options with a ploy or a strategy, but that has no guarantees whatsoever. Open intelligence *does* have a guarantee.

If for instance people had allergies that they wanted to have treated, they could go through all the tests using different foods to try to understand how to cure the allergy. The resulting treatment could work in some way, but it will never give them any sense of complete total well-being. Proceeding with that line of treatment is a total shot in the dark; however, by the power of open intelligence-assurance in your own experience, you get to see what the afflictive states of your own body and mind really are—the potency of open intelligence itself.

It's the beginning and the end of your own health and the beginning and the end of a healthy human society. Take the radical plunge that completely releases all hope and fear. Within that you'll know what to do and how to act. That has to be the basis.

SEE WHAT'S REALLY IN THERE

There's no back door: it's either one hundred commitment or not. By the power of short moments, open intelligence will be obviously continuous. It already is continuous; it's just that by the power of these short moments, which are radically simple, it becomes obvious that it has always already been continuous.

Someone had commented about open intelligence not being present for them when they were relating with the opposite sex. Whether you're presently relating with the opposite sex or not, there can never be a full-on relationship with anyone without open intelligence. You can't fool yourself. You could make all kinds of assumptions about open intelligence not being present, but where exactly did it go? You can't get out of it: if you decide to rely on it, *that* is fueled by open intelligence; if you decide not to rely on it, *that* is fueled by open intelligence; if you feel yourself in a downhill spiral, *that* is fueled by open intelligence. That's the magic touch right there; there's no way out and no way in.

There are all these states going on, and it really needs to get to the level where you can look at what is going on in the pits of despair and every realm that you have ever visited. As all these subtle things are floating around—the jealousies, how miserable you can make yourself, this, that and the other thing—look at it specifically. "What about that jealousy? Who am I jealous of?" Then, sit down and write it out the most horrible way that could ever play out. "I'm so jealous of that one. My gosh, look at them; look at what they're doing and look at what I'm not doing. They're a shining star and I'm a lowly nothing." Whatever it might be, get down into the depths of your feelings about that. "I'm no good, I've never been any good and I'll never be good. This is such a rotten life. I can't stand it. What the hell am I doing here; get me out of here." All the while remain as you are, no matter what's going on. Get down with all the data. If you really need to communicate about the data, go to the very basis and see how far you can go. See how miserable you can make yourself in your own data stream!

If you see somebody else and they're acting bizarre, and you can't detach yourself from what they're thinking, write about what's going on with them. "Oh, they must be a real weirdo, a manic depressive. Who knows what they're thinking. They're probably thinking this about me and that about the other one." See how far you can take it. Instead of just skating on the surface with all these little butterfly sets of data, see what's really in there. When you look, you find more and more that whatever you're looking at, there isn't anything there. Where is it?

Develop the intensity of these really awful, horrid data. That's the real open intelligence power right there. You're not indulging them; indulging them means mindlessly going off on a whole story of data. Instead, use negative data as a support in maintaining open intelligence while you vomit forth all the negativity. In this way they're known to be the surge of power, and the only experience you're left with is the surge of power. This is the distinction: indulgence is just mindless regurgitation of data with no escape, but using negative data as a support is to maintain open intelligence, inseparable from the power surge of data.

THE POWER OF DISCERNMENT

Many of us are afraid of our data streams. We're trying to be nice, and we want the nice data, because they are the ones that show us we have an identity that is okay. We've learned that if we don't have nice data, then there's something wrong with us. At some point though we have to face the truth, and an easy way to do that is to purposely confront all data in your own ex-

127

perience. Otherwise, we only do things that hint at these types of data, like watching a movie such as *The Terminator* or *Friday the 13th* or something like that. By diverting ourselves we get to have all kinds of excited states, but they're not really connected with us.

Afflictive states hold immense potency to really break out of all conventional ideas about how to proceed. They allow us to break through our little teeny voice into the potency of truly beneficial speech. Until then we just try to play with different strategies. Earlier I mentioned one of the strategies: intuition. If there is a strong force and a weak force in the physical world, then you could say that intuition is the weak force. It's just another point of view. We might say, "Oh, now I've got my intuition; this is the answer," but the first question to ask would be how many times it has been the right answer. Intuition is just another point of view, and we draw wisdom and profundity from open intelligence itself—not from fleeting intuitions. We rely on what is stable, permanent, unchanging and indestructible. There can be insights, thoughts, emotions, sensations, whatever they are, but we rely on the power of open intelligence.

All of us have been through a very wide range of all kinds of powerful, negative and neutral states already, and we have tried all kinds of strategies in relation to them. We know what the whole game plan is; we've all had enough afflictive states and we know what they are. By the power of open intelligence we get to go beyond all our preconceived definitions that we've been using about all these afflictive states and other states. We get to rest firm and solid in the power of open intelligence, rather than in all the preconceived definitions.

In these very afflictive states we find real power—the power of discernment and the power to accomplish any beneficial activity we set out to accomplish. These are real powers of real human beings carrying open intelligence identity to the maximum degree.

Value Letters from Participants

I used to value my intellect and learned knowledge. It made me feel slightly better about myself if I knew more facts about everything than anyone else. I was very adept at amassing truckloads of secondhand information, and I became expert at proving that my secondhand knowledge was better and more important than other people's. There was so much effort, so much struggling to polish this thinnest of veneers, but it only obscured a life overwhelmed by cynicism, negativity, depression and boredom.

When I first came to my first Balanced View open meeting, even though I was dragged along like an unwilling child, I was immediately struck by the disarming and gentle nature of the training. My cynicism and criticism were given no fuel to feed on; my cynicism just happily bubbled and festered by itself as I was told to "just show up" and "test the simple suggestions in my own experience," and I consider myself greatly fortunate that I was able to do so. I tested these instructions, and despite my rabid resistance and reluctance, by just showing up and listening to the talks I noticed something earth shattering: for the briefest of moments I was okay.

If such simple and easy to follow instructions produced the results that were promised, what would happen if I availed myself even more of the support offered by the Four Mainstays? So, this is what I did. I listened to downloads and participated in trainings continuously. I served the community as much as I was able, and when I could not recognize open intelligence, I sought the advice of my trainers.

Many times in the beginning that would just involve me crying in the corner complaining to my trainers whilst I wallowed in self-pity and misery—two of my life's most faithful companions. The knowledge that I had support, and taking the support when needed, were essential for me in gaining initial confidence in open intelligence when it seemed otherwise impossible. In relying on the Four Mainstays, gradually increasing relaxation and ease were recognized in more and more of my experience.

My experience remained exactly the same: I was bored and fairly miserable most of the time, but instead of being despondent, I was amused and pleased to recognize elation, as it increasingly appeared. I came to understand that being able to rely on open intelligence has got NOTHING to do with a change in the display of my data. My misery, anger, frustration, boredom, apathy and depression were the greatest gifts imaginable, always bringing me home—sometimes by the scruff of the neck—to open intelligence in each shining short moment. You can keep your happiness and bliss; I know where true open intelligence is located!

One of the most skillful and powerful aspects of these amazing teachings is the process of participants answering questions and then sharing their letters. This part of the training always brings up the greatest afflictive states in me, and for that I am incredibly grateful. My reliance on the Four Mainstays has given me a life beyond imagining, and this is only the beginning of something so powerful and marvelous, I cannot comprehend what's in store for the world. But I know it's going to be beyond awesome. Thank you; I bow down to your brilliance; you are amazing. Love and service forever.

SECOND SHARE

My old ideas about perfection always included the dream about the perfect partner for happiness, safety and completeness, but that never worked out. I also longed for and searched for the perfect way of using my time, gifts and talents in a beneficial way, combined with a strong longing to express myself without knowing what it was that I wanted to express. I dedicated myself to spiritual practices, where the goal was a perfectly balanced and refined body and mind, with the hope that finally the way would be free for my mind to be blown open and free.

With immense gratitude I can see that the perfection and relief I wished for was effortlessly fulfilled already in the first short moment of open intelligence. Step by step, walking with the Four Mainstays, a stable recognition of open intelligence has unfolded, and there is no way to stop the beneficial force of open intelligence—no limits, no beginning and no end. Bright light, increasingly experienced as brighter and brighter.

The connectivity with my trainer frees me from every uncertainty in action, every impulse to emphasize data. She empowers me to recognize myself and others as limitless capacity and expansion. My trainer's wide open manifestation of unconditional love and open intelligence is a beautiful inspiration. Reaching out to her has been an effective way to shift my self-centered identification with data (body, mind, thoughts, emotions, memories, experiences, etc.) to open intelligence.

The training is always new, even if I have done many of the trainings many times. As the light shines brighter, it enlightens the text in new ways. And Candice, you are incredible. In every training with you that I have had the fortune to participate in, each day I have asked myself, "The training is already so complete, powerful, and beautiful; how could it go further than this?" But of course I know that each time you will go further! Your training is the force of open intelligence itself, in every moment complete, fulfilled and still an infinite, sparkling adventure, full on.

The Four Mainstays demonstrate the vision of a open intelligence society here and now, and have convinced me through my own direct experience of the joy, pleasure, effectiveness and results of open intelligence teamwork, the power in allowing myself and others to be as we are—effortless togetherness when we take responsibility for our data, true connection and pure love in wide open perception. In every data is absolute satisfaction, simultaneous inseparability and self-release. In the beneficial force of open intelligence, recognized in relaxed open-heartedness, nothing is needed, everything is possible, accessible and inescapable. With love, forever grateful, in service for the benefit of all.

Day Eight

BLOWING OPEN PLEASURE

The Written Text and Commentary

(The written text is in bold)
(The commentary is in normal script.)

Blissful pleasure without cause is natural identity, potent benefit its display. So simple, right here in the current data: blissful pleasure without cause. The fundamental identity, the essence right here in the current data, whatever that is.

The blast blows everything into wide open intelligence, devouring all pleasure-related data in great bliss. Just that—the very precious, greatly fortunate introduction to open intelligence. It devours everything in great bliss. Just allowing it to be *as it is*, everything is devoured in great bliss.

In open intelligence, pleasure is no longer associated only with specific activities. Moment-to-moment we go along increasingly each moment unveiling more pleasure. We start to see, whoa, it doesn't matter what I'm thinking, what I'm feeling, what I'm sensing, what I'm experiencing—everything is an emphatic statement of bliss, without any idea about bliss. It is not a blissful state that needs to look a certain way. *Everything* is a statement of bliss.

No longer directed like puppets to strive for pleasure, carefree beneficial qualities and activities spontaneously emerge. When we're driven by our pleasure motive, seeking pleasure and satisfaction in so many things, then we miss the bliss motive in each moment. We miss the inherent bliss right here in the current data. In terror—self-arising bliss; in just allowing the terror to be *as it is*—self-arising bliss; in exhilaration—self-arising bliss; in burnout and boredom—self-arising bliss; in lethargy and fixation—self-arising bliss; in complete freedom from all absolutes—self-arising bliss. It doesn't matter how we dress it up—naked bliss. This frees up our energy, because we're no longer always seeking pleasure with our energy.

The great cheering up of society in open intelligence uninstalls the puppet program of continuous pleasure-seeking and simultaneously installs unending bliss. The game is over. No pleasure to seek anywhere but right here. It's up to us. We run on a program we installed ourselves; we're responsible for our own descriptions. No one else can make us have them, so we're never a victim of any of our data—not ever, never a victim. In instinctive open intelligence we give up our right to be a victim: victimized by all those data society forced on us or our family or whoever we're blaming. We're self-responsible in instinctive open intelligence; we uninstall the victim program and simultaneously upload bliss.

Blissful pleasure is always fully loaded in all circumstances, the operating system of identity. Blissful pleasure is always fully loaded in all circumstances whatever they are, the operating system of identity. It's very common that when introduced to instinctive open intelligence, one of the first questions that comes up is, "Well, what about war; what about child abuse," or what about whatever examples it might be. The only way to overcome all negativity of all kinds individually and collectively is in open intelligence. Just as instinctive open intelligence makes all special states obsolete in the individual, thus it does so in society. It's not rocket science; it's very easy.

Just as we lose track of things that happened long ago, so society can lose complete track of ever being involved in suffering. It's up to us individually. We lose track of all memories of suffering in instinctive open intelligence, because everything is self-arising bliss. In this way we go beyond all causal effort, we go beyond cause and effect as a mechanism for making us feel the way we do. By the power of our own open intelligence everything is normalized.

Causality is a datum, period. Someone asked me recently, "What do you do about self-loathing?" Open intelligence—that's what you do about self-loathing! In self-loathing there is self-arising bliss.

Truly real pleasure does not come from a cause. That's the wake-up call right there. Pleasure does not come from a cause.

Open intelligence is pleasure's magnificent mate. Very easy, very direct, right here, whatever we're thinking, whatever we're feeling, whatever we're experiencing—self-arising bliss. If it's high or low or in between, the equalness and evenness of self-arising bliss.

Since open intelligence is not a product of any condition, it is delightfully and potently present, as this and this and this and this and this.

Simply resting without contrivance in open intelligence, our full force and pleasure-power is spontaneously obvious. So simple, nothing to get, nothing to change, nothing to do.

All data is nothing but open intelligence pleasure enjoying itself. Just you, right here, as you are, open intelligence-pleasure enjoying itself.

Open intelligence deletes forever the datum that pleasure comes only from causal circumstances such as food, money, sex, work, romance, friendships, family, entertainment and so forth. Nothing subtle, nothing overt, each moment equally self-arising bliss. All terms—subtle, overt, boring, exhilarating—all of them equally and evenly self-arising bliss, nowhere to go, nothing to do, the forever fuel station.

Thus, empowered to truly enjoy all of these with an attitude of carefree openness and responsibility, we carry on living with great ease no matter what comes about. When there's no pleasure to get to, nothing to derive some time in the future, everything is freed up in beneficial qualities and activities. No need to sit around forever enjoying some blissful state; bliss embodied in every single moment, no matter what it's looking like.

Benefit, prosperity and generosity replace constant lack and search for satisfaction and fulfillment. So easy and simple, a very direct equation: no pleasure to find in the future. It's right here in the panic attack, in the terror, in the anxiety, in the imagined state of perfect bliss, the imagined state of perfect open intelligence—each moment equal, no fabricated framework to put together in order to enjoy oneself. Complete release from the prison of the pleasure motive and of looking for something sometime in the future. This moment stripped naked, just *as it is*.

When a sensory twinge or urge is automatically described as sexual or erotic, open intelligence ignorance holds sway, unfolding a confusing story about these data. How many times have we had an erotic urge and then had a whole story unfold about it? Maybe you just realized you ended up with someone for fifty years because of that! By misunderstanding the fundamental nature of experience, all kinds of stories unfold. By correctly understanding and instinctively recognizing the nature of every single thing—the actual identity of every single datum— complete pleasure is derived. No confusion any longer; you are able to sort things out, because in the confusion is found no confusion. In confusion itself is found open intelligence. In the very labeling of confusion, of fabricating some kind of confused state, is self-arising bliss. No confusion any longer because in confusion, there's no confusion.

135

From the moment of birth, we teach ourselves to describe certain bodily sensations, thoughts, emotions and other experiences as sexual or erotic by nature. Whatever we do, it's okay; just relax, get to know yourself exactly as you are.

When this data is granted an independent nature, it creates chaos and extremely confused states that are lifelong. It's okay, take it easy.

By the time puberty is reached, complete confusion sets in. By misunderstanding the nature of identity, by puberty complete confusion sets in. We have no idea what's going on.

Puberty is actually the period for fully recognizing, launching and spontaneously demonstrating the great power of benefit to be displayed by a mature human. When the potent sexual urges and surges of childhood and adolescence are misidentified as real and independently existent, a lifetime of bewilderment and diminished energy ensues. We simply didn't learn this; however, we're our own parent right now. Open intelligence is where it's at. We always have an indestructible family home, and we can rely on that without fail to sort out any of the limiting confusions we have about anything. In open intelligence we clear it all up. As we do, we naturally feel more energetic; it's just the way it is. We don't have anything to keep in place anymore, no states we need to avoid in order to feel good. We find the real feel-good, just as it is right here.

If open intelligence is trained up as the nature of all erotic or sexual viewpoints, then open intelligence is discovered to be the potent erotic situation we feel driven to find. Right here, whatever you're thinking about, whatever image you have, it's the perfect erotic situation. So get real; that's where it all begins.

Only open intelligence is the basis for enduring relationship of any kind; otherwise, all relating—individual and collective—is fundamentally driven to indulge, avoid or replace

the great variety of erotic or sexual or other data. This is very, very simple; the open intelligence and data. What do we do with the data? We have four choices: indulge, avoid, replace or clarify. This is the basic education for everyone, no one left out—the means to overcome all negativity of all kinds, right here in this moment.

The erotic impulse itself, like all data, rests in self-arising pleasure and bliss. Nothing to look for; it's all right here.

These are the most potent and profound of the potent and profound instructions. Open intelligence and data in every single moment, indivisibly together as self-arising bliss.

These instructions contain the most essential point, because radiant pleasure appears directly. This is your identity, so you just carry on in a powerfully beneficial way. Not contriving anything, clarity luminosity appears as direct experience; the transparent here-and-now undoes itself in the great release of pure pleasure. Nothing to get hold of, a continuous flow, by any name.

Open intelligence-pleasure and bliss is the ultimate indestructible vehicle, the outshining of data in open intelligence. Right here, whatever it is—the anxiety, the exhilaration, the no thoughts, the thoughts, the desire, no desire, the confusion, the lack of confusion, self-arising bliss, the young, the old, the ugly, the beautiful, the in-between—self-arising bliss.

Open intelligence bright energy, self-aware, original potent intelligence, instinctive pleasure and benefit shine forth immediately, as the current moment. Nothing complicated; you just are as you are, no before and after, no fix-up needed.

No need to wait for a result to ripen later. Right here, just as you are, perfect accord.

This liberates here-and-now. It is the force that frees here-and-now in blissful accord. Your own current label is the force that frees everything in blissful accord.

Data arise as open intelligence-pleasure already, so as a result data are already liberated. Liberated in a continuous flow.

Instinctively recognize the open intelligence view and data are beloved self-arising pleasure. All cleared up, just like that.

Day Eight Talk

It doesn't matter what the datum is, each one of them is equally endowed with pleasure and bliss. When we are confused about this, we think that certain data are the source of erotic pleasure, but we'll clear that up completely now! The whole notion of describing something and putting it into a fixed framework limits pleasure, because pleasure is in self-arising bliss.

I am married, and I'm in a monogamous relationship. I have two children, both around forty years old, and eight grandchildren. Like everyone else I have been subjected to all of society's data about sex and everything else. I know exactly where everybody's coming from in terms of avoiding, indulging, replacing and clarifying sexual data.

The clarification of data as self-arising pleasure and bliss is really the zenith of erotic experience. Unless that is so in our individual experience, we have never really taken a lover. Each experience is that union of open intelligence and data. This may sound corny, but it really is that way. With everything I've been through in terms of being married, having children, raising children, having grandchildren, living life in all kinds of ways—there have been many, many things that have occurred, just like with everyone else. However, the full-fledged showing up for that, in, of, as, and through open intelligence, without open intelligence being confined to any particular thing or situation, is just the greatest erotic experience that could ever be imagined.

SELF-ARISING BLISS

Whatever your own experience is, it is the source of bliss and erotic pleasure. It's really impossible to ever have any kind of satisfactory sexual relating with anyone else without fully entering into that. All data, no matter what they are, are equally self-arising bliss. So many times we learn that there are data that limit bliss and pleasure—desire, no desire, boredom, exhilaration, fatigue, lethargy, honeymoons, the wedding night, tons of money, no money, living in a cave, living in a mansion—whatever they are. We get all these ideas about where pleasure is or where it will come from. However, whatever our experience is, whether it's the terror of the moment or the joy of the moment, allowing everything to be exactly *as it is* with no special situations or special states is the real act of indivisibility. That makes life very easy.

In that is such tremendous freedom, because everything—desire, jealousy, pride, ignorance, anger—is completely freed up by allowing it all to be *as it is*. The height of erotic pleasure is allowing all of that to be. Erotic pleasure is fulfilled in our own data—whatever is arising right now. Sometimes people feel uncomfortable if they're riddled with desire, and sometimes people feel uncomfortable if they have no desire; however, it just is whatever it is. In open intelligence we get to be familiar with the full range of data without making it into a description of who we are. Many of us feel driven by sexual urges—as if we didn't have any control—but this is a datum, too. We might as well simply relax and enjoy the inherent bliss in every single datum.

The built-in birth control, so to speak, is in open intelligence. Real birth control never comes about from a pill or any other device. We can think that it has, but it never really does. We have within us a way to control our population. No one ever need be sexually out of control; inherently, no one is ever sexually out of control. That is the basic sex education that we need, and without that all kinds of things will play out.

THE HEIGHT OF INTIMACY

We have all kinds of relationships to our data, depending on who we are. Some have a propensity to indulge, others to avoid, others to replace, others to clarify. Our own sexuality and erotic drive are really the fundamental drive to rely on open intelligence in order to sort everything out.

From the time we were very small, most of us have trained ourselves to have certain data sets about different bodily sensations and to identify those as somehow sexual, but who says they have to be sexual? Where is that a law? We have the complete power to interpret our experience in any way we want to.

If we interpret it as sexual, that's a choice. If we get locked down in that, that's a choice.

I could look out at a large group of people, and everyone would look totally desirable and pleasant to me, and for me that's no problem. Every single person I see looks great to me. A lot of times we restrict ourselves and restrain our natural responsiveness, because we get choked up in ideas of what appropriate conduct is and what appropriate thoughts, emotions, sensations or other experiences are. The most intimate we can ever be is with our own experience, whatever that is. That's really the height of intimacy. Whatever our experience is, whether we deem it sexual or not, that is an offering of pure pleasure.

Depending on our circumstances we all have different attitudes about sexual experience. Whatever our attitudes are, they are entirely circumstantial. Some of us grow up and we feel restricted about data related to erotic pleasure, and we feel they might be scary or even terrifying for different reasons. Or it could be the opposite extreme: we're completely out of control, and if we have a sexual desire we think we have to act on it. Whatever these data are, they can only be resolved and brought into complete accord and intimacy through open intelligence.

Whether you're in a sexual relationship or not, it's okay to have erotic pleasure, because that is the natural drive of all human beings. It's the essence of fulfillment in each moment. By letting sexual desire be *as it is* as a datum, we come into satisfactory sexual experience, sometimes for the first time. Sex isn't a special datum and the erotic drive is not a special datum—they are equal to every other datum. All these data really are uncontrollable, and trying to manage erotic or any other data leads to a feeling of dissatisfaction, like there's something more to get.

NORMALIZING ALL DATA

There are no longer impulses and drives that seem abnormal. That means everything is normalized, and it's normalized in great pleasure and bliss, where there's no special act that is needed to create pleasure or bliss. Any kind of sexual relating can be really enjoyable, because it doesn't require any special set of data. There's complete freedom. Things come up such as, "Oh, well, I have to be thinking this," or "I better not be thinking that," or "I'm a weirdo," or "What about all those things that happened earlier on when I was a kid, or when I was sexually assaulted," or whatever it was. All these things might be problems for us, and they might appear when we're involved in sexual experience. All of our attitudes about sex will come up when we get together with someone else, and they'll start to play themselves out exactly where we don't want them to—in bed!

So, maybe we sign up for a tantric workshop, and we'll see how to do it and what to do and what to think and how to ask them to do that and tell them not to do that—really, oh my God! I've never been to one of those workshops, but you could say that I've held my own!

By allowing all these data to be as they are, we relax in the realm of sexual relating. We can really take it or leave it. That's the way it's supposed to be—take it or leave it—not controlled by it, but not avoiding it either. Encountering everything fully and directly. We each have our own little scenario we've created about a perfect sexual experience, but whatever that scenario is, it'll never work out. If it's some kind of scenario about someone needing to look a certain way to be sexually attractive or a sexually satisfying experience will never work out. It doesn't matter how attractive the other person is, that's never going to make your sexual experience unendingly satisfying.

In open intelligence, sex becomes satisfying—just like everything else is satisfying. It's normalized; it is not some kind of thing to avoid or to impulsively indulge or something that needs to be replaced with something else because the urge is too great or too little. By the power of your own open intelligence, in coming together with someone else you can learn a lot about yourself.

But guess what? You don't even need anyone else. You're sexual, strong and free exactly as you are without anyone else. There's a lot of data involving your sexual twinges and urges that can be explored with yourself, and if you want to do that without involving anyone else, you can. We each have complete freedom in that regard, no matter what we've learned. The whole purview of our data is just within our own view, so it's entirely up to us to normalize it. No one else can do it for us. We can't go to someone else who will tell us exactly how to do that; we can only see how to do that in our own experience, in the reach and range of all of our own data, no matter what they are.

REAL FREEDOM

In this way, every moment becomes one of erotic pleasure. Some people like sex and some people don't, but so what? It really doesn't matter; take it or leave it. This is an attitude of carefree openness. When all the urges, surges, twinges, thoughts and emotions are all sorted out in the bliss of open intelligence, then we have real freedom individually, and we have real freedom as a society. There's no mistake about it, there really isn't.

People go through all kinds of things in a relationship, and to have a framework of expectation for yourself or others related to sexuality is totally a dead end. If you have some kind of expectation of another person or of yourself, all of that has to be sorted out. There are all these expectations, all these drives, all these impulses, all the fantasies, all the thoughts, emotions and sensations. By not trying to fix them up, not trying to shove them into a certain little form, letting everything be *as it is*, that's where the real freedom is found.

Have you ever noticed that in actual erotic involvement, whoa, the data really go wild? "Whoops, better not be having that one! I'm thinking about that horrible thing that happened when I was a kid," and so on. Whatever it is, let it be *as it is*. This will open up the ability to really be completely at ease. You could look at everyone and think they look great, or you could think that you would never want to get into bed with anybody ever again, but both are equal. There's no mystery involved at all. It is very straightforward: basic self-knowledge, right here.

In that immediate self-knowledge of the pure pleasure of the here-and-now, all these things get sorted out. We find that we've really been subjected to all kinds of social injunctions about erotic desire, and they come flooding in from everywhere—from religion, education, the criminal justice system. But we take responsibility. In open intelligence all our gender roles and everything else that we've imagined as related to erotic desire or involvement is completely normalized. It's fine for everyone to look good to you or not—women and men or a particular one of either gender; it just doesn't matter, take it or leave it.

By normalizing all your data in the great bliss of open intelligence, you know exactly how to proceed. You know what it means to really involve another human being in your life in that way, and you can approach it with great responsibility. That can only come about by normalizing all your data in open intelligence. This is the way to be responsible. It's not a mystery: you take responsibility for yourself and all your own data, whatever they are in this moment. That's the greatest act of pleasure, right there. If you're in a relationship with someone else and both of you are always wanting to have sex at the exact same moment, then you're really outside the norm, because very rarely is it going to be that way. It may not be that way at all; in fact, it probably isn't.

There's a lot of normalization that can occur within oneself without involving anyone else, and when that step is made to involve someone else, through the self-responsibility of open intelligence we understand exactly what we're getting into. Those impulses and drives may have led us in all kinds of directions, but now they don't anymore. We still have them, but we don't feel driven by them. In fact, open intelligence opens up the full range of erotic desire and the full range of pleasure as being self-evident in every datum.

So, we can just relax and enjoy life—take it in stride, not driven to do any particular thing, always knowing that open intelligence will guide us and show us a responsible and enjoyable course of action.

Value Letters from Participants

FIRST SHARE

I could never seem to feel natural about my sexual longings, whether I was fulfilling my longings or not. I wished that I could have sexual intimacy with the women that I most desired, and by doing so I might somehow finally be relieved of being pulled around by sexual desire. Although intellectually it was clear to me that this strategy would never really work, I was still a slave to it. I saw that no matter how much sex I had, and no matter how attractive my partner was, I would never reach a point of satisfaction. This made me feel trapped: being compelled by sexual desire and at the same time seeing the futility of following through on it in an attempt to bring any lasting satisfaction to me or anybody else.

I concluded that sexual desire was basically a manifestation of my impurity. I felt ashamed and disgusted with myself when lusting after a woman. I wished I could just be happy and satisfied as I was without needing someone to have sex with me. I was disgusted with myself for not being able to overcome this.

I finally found the ability to allow intense compelling perceptions of sexual desire to wash through me without my trying to do anything about them. This taught me that sexual desire did not require me to do anything in order for me to be free and uncontrived in its midst. From then on the ongoing appearances of sexual desire never really disturbed me again, and I was for the first time in my life able to take it or leave it. This was such a huge relief.

Last time I was home, good old friends of mine were asking me about my love life and did not know how to relate to the fact that I hadn't had one for years! So, I went on to explain how I used to be so compelled by sexual desire, that I had felt like a slave to it and that this was one of the main things propelling me to have intimate relationships in the first place. I explained that I had found that it no longer had that power over me, and I just relished the freedom of not being propelled into relationship based on such a primitive drive. They could all completely relate and wanted to know the exact mechanism by which they could also find the way to no longer be a slave to sexual desire

Everybody wants peace in their lives; there just needs to be the initial bridge of communication which helps them to see what that peace is, how it can be found and what it means in terms of real life situations.

SECOND SHARE

I've learned that sources of pleasure were things like eating good food, desserts or having a tasty drink; lying in a hammock after completing some work; being happy with not knowing what the future will be and feeling adventurous about it; making a decision and knowing it's the right one, even when others don't understand or disagree; being completely "in the moment" when having sex; having an orgasm; seeing that the person I'm having sex with is really enjoying it.

Concerning erotic surges and urges, I had learned that viewpoints such as those are okay if you hide them well and only show them to an intimate partner, and *never* reveal what took place in the bedroom. With a partner I've learned that I need to look sexy, only show specific parts or angles of my body and always have a sexy look on my face.

I've learned that women's bodies are really kind of sexier than men's. I've learned that *thinking* about having sex with women is wild and cool, but that it's not normal to talk about that with anyone or to actually *have* sex with a woman. I've learned that for a man to want to have sex with me I need to look nice and harmless and move my body in a smooth and sexy way. I had learned that if you see an attractive man and get a sexual impulse, that's life telling you to act on it, and you should.

There was someone special that I really liked, and I suspected that he was "the one." Once I was first introduced to the Balanced View training and I gained more confidence in open intelligence, all the emotions went wild: I had so many fantasies about him, sexual and other, and I planned for the moment I'd ask him out. I thought the time to ask him out would be perfect after I'd finished the Twelve Empowerments—I'd be perfectly stable and our relationship would be just right and that would make things easier.

Well, I never asked him out. He's beautiful and really cool, but I could see clearly that the best decision would be for me to gain more confidence in open intelligence before entering a sexual relationship. Instinctive open intelligence guided me to this decision, no mystery involved. That was really powerful to see my strength and my ability to go against my data regarding relationships that I wanted to have.

Today's training and text have been such a profound and opening clarification for me. I'd never before thought of sexual desire as just an aspect of the bliss of open intelligence. It has really seemed up until now like sexual desire has its own identity and power, but wow, how simple life can be: you can take it or leave it; you have sex or you don't, but either way you're perfectly fine. That's so cool! And to think that pleasure doesn't come from sex, but that it's the other way around—that the bliss of open intelligence is the basis of pleasurable data like sex, wow, everything is turned upside down.

I've been taking short moments with sexual desire and I really love normalizing these thoughts with the piercing force of open intelligence—all the nasty, insane, weird, I–should-be-in-a-hospital thoughts. Ha-ha, I'm not a victim of them; they're present but they have absolutely NO power over me. I'm so excited to continue normalizing everything, in the same way that yesterday I looked at my anger and helplessness and saw how far I could take that. Now I can also see how weird my thoughts about sex can get, but that is completely normalized by relying on open intelligence.

My trainer has helped me understand that I'm not at the whim of a desire to be with a man, and that through gaining confidence in open intelligence I'll have a much more stable foundation for starting a relationship with someone.

Thank you for a fantastic, hilarious, super-empowering and super-informative training and text that have helped me to a much more easeful life.

Day Nine

POTENCY

Written Text and Commentary

Many people have mentioned to me, "I'm going to be going home after this retreat, and these sexual data streams come up when I'm not here, and there isn't someone right next to me I can reach out to and get help." Well, we're always available 24/7. The website is always there. Pick up your phone, call someone and check in. We now also offer 24/7 Live Support on our www.balancedview.com website so that participants can be in touch with a trainer any time of the day or night. If you need some grounding in open intelligence regarding your course of action in any situation, it's always available. If you're feeling a little fuzzy for any reason, there is support always available, 24 hours a day.

Even though this text is quite long, these are very important words. It will clear up everything that you might be questioning or you might want to show it up to someone else. It just clears up a lot of mistaken ideas in a simple way.

The vast bliss expanse, very potent intelligence—the most profound of the profound intelligence pervading all data and all fields of knowledge—is right here. Right here in the current datum. **Potent intelligence is accessed only through non-contrivance of data;** it means you don't have to fix them up in any certain way; **allowing all data to flow on by, like a line drawn in mid-air—pristine sky in pristine sky, without object or support.**

This freedom is found in the equal bliss-pleasure of all data, the opening of human society to a new way of life. Each moment of open intelligence prevents the return to societal

suffering. Yes, each moment of open intelligence is that powerful.

Non-contrivance, letting data flow on by, is the installation
process of potent intelligence for society, individually and
collectively. We see that we are absolutely okay, powerful;
open intelligence is always on. This potent software is running brilliantly as it is already engineered into our nature,
making it impossible for outdated programs to operate, giving a thorough cut to their energy supply in each short moment.

The short moment expands to long moments and then days,
months, years, or even lifetimes of potent benefit. This is our
birthright and direction. All other information we have
learned is incorrect and inadequate.

Very potent open intelligence's outcomes are exceptional
and always provide unimaginable benefit and gifted human
life, providing each moment the pure potency of practical
clear intelligence. The complete power in each datum
soothes all tensions and stories rolling this way and that with
their innate indestructible stability. Have you ever noticed
that? Data have a story that runs this way and that. No matter
which way it runs, open intelligence is running the show. Simple open intelligence relieves the burden of causal descriptions of the here-and-now, illuminating insight into reality.

Our past understanding of sexuality and erotics is just
another program that can be quickly uninstalled after years
of laborious installation, radically uninstalled in open intelligence's thorough blowing open of continuous pleasure and
sanity in all moments.

How people experience and express data that are described
as sexual or erotic, or any data for that matter, especially
the feelings or urges related to pleasure, is so simple after

149

all. This includes not only the state of arousal and anticipation of pleasure, but also the attempt through various means to incite and satisfy those feelings. All data, clearly knowing, powerfully enacted by open intelligence—that is the basis. To know it, know open intelligence. **By the potency of open intelligence alone, all these attitudes and incidents—past, present and future—are sorted out for the benefit of all.** Sorted out in yourself by the power of open intelligence. This gives you discerning insight, absolute discrimination into the nature of your own conduct.

Totally open intelligence always arises with the emphatic gesture of the benefit of all. The gesture of gratitude and respect ensures the benefit and deep caring for everyone we connect with. Inherent to open intelligence, the gesture of benefit. Just by the simple practice of open intelligence, there is uncontrived benefit. **Open intelligence automatically instantaneously asks without ever thinking the question, "How will this impulse to pleasure be an energy that benefits all in its expression?"** Whatever it is, whatever that instinct to pleasure, instantaneously the question is asked, "How will this be of benefit to all?"

The pleasure drive is based on a program we have been running comprised of thoughts, emotions, sensations and other experience that seem to be associated with pleasure. When we examine them from the perspective of open intelligence, we cannot find a location, really, where they are coming from, or even where they are now, or where they end sometime in the future. We cannot say where it is or how it got there, how it could be a source of power or influence that might control us. We find only open intelligence there, as its sole support. **This is conclusive experiential evidence that the data streams of pleasure, or any named datum, cannot be found to have an independent power or force to make anyone or anything act in any particular way. Rather, it is like space pouring into space, light pouring into light.**

Sexual data, like all others, have no nature independent of open intelligence. By relying on the blast of open intelligence rather than on sexual data, we unleash a healthy, vast erotic view that is filled with enormous beneficial energy. The blind bondage of sexual programming is set free in an expanse of super-pleasure at all times, night and day. The metaphors are chosen very carefully. Even in the indulgence, avoidance or replacement of erotic data, we carefully rely on short moments and the other Mainstays and their clear power to expose the benefit of all in the course of our actions. Open intelligence is so natural and succinct just like that. The power of the benefit of all is in each short moment with no contrivance whatsoever.

Seeking sexual pleasure and orgasmic relief as an end in itself slips into moment-to-moment pleasure with no cause. This gives us true erotic dignity, integrity and great freedom of choice. Secret erotic lifestyles that leave us shamed and questioning our basic worth are opened up to open intelligence potency and wise input that adds to the ease of all situations and the secure knowledge that the future is optimistic regardless of its offering. Whatever that secret pursuit is, you know, the one that you won't tell anyone about, the one you don't even want to know you're thinking? Even that one is a blazing expression of open intelligence. Right here let it be *as it is*. Even take the next step and share it with someone else; write it down and share it. Phew! Not a secret anymore. Nothing is secret to open intelligence anyway. Normalize everything in the great potent intelligence.

Avoidance of erotic thoughts, emotions, sensations and other experiences is relaxed into pure, spontaneous, open, indivisible open intelligence. Sexual and erotic excellence resides only in open intelligence spontaneity, nowhere else.

Deep-seated data burst open to instinctive love-bliss power. Love's super-potency is the unavoidable bind of pleasure found in the potent open intelligence view within all data. No point from which to view in open intelligence's view. Have you ever noticed that? It's really impossible to ever keep a datum, so why would we be living from one. You can never keep it; where is it?

Instinctively, potent open intelligence displays immediate powerful benefit, right here. In open intelligence is discovered the fulfillment of love, pleasure and intimacy, right here. Open intelligence is the dependable means to initiate and satisfy indestructible pleasure in all dimensions of living. Again, right here; nowhere to get to. **Now it is possible to enjoy human sexuality and all of life in a free, relaxed and responsible way.**

In the great permission of open intelligence, all data are normalized; the erotic impulse is entirely elective and selective based on spontaneous natural mutual ethics that serve the benefit of all. All these words mean only "open intelligence." Right here, that's where spontaneous natural ethics can be found. **Open intelligence enables human society to subsume primitive sexual drives and urges in an ultimate erotic burst of unbridled benefit, prosperity and generosity.** This is what we are really getting at, right here.

Open intelligence is relied upon to display its immediate power of pure pleasure and total erotic fulfillment, equalizing all erotic and other data—positive, negative and neutral—normalizing all data just as they are. By normalizing all data just as they are, unleashing an intelligence that can never ever be accessed otherwise, only by non-contrivance, letting all data be exactly as they are.

In actual erotic experience, the experience of pleasure seeking, **spontaneously rely on the open intelligence blast as all data flow on by, none better or worse. Freedom in immediate sexual data is the only source of true intimacy, satisfaction and fulfillment.** Freedom in the immediate perception of all data is indeed the only source of true intimacy, satisfaction and fulfillment. **In this way, we open completely within all data to responsive erotic play and a potent surge of pleasure and benefit of all that spontaneously flows throughout all aspects of our life.** Wow, and we thought it required foreplay! **We really get intimate with all data and this allows us true societal intimacy—personally and collectively. We're all running on the same super-open intelligence bandwidth.**

In any moment, all notions of open intelligence are blown open, without any effort at all, releasing unparalleled beneficial power and ease of action. Open intelligence is the super current surge of data, and now it is this surge, never settling down in anything, always swelling with vitality, potency and indestructibility. The bright view of open intelligence is present in all data, so simple, so easy. Nowhere else, nowhere to get to, nothing to do.

Instinctively recognizing the inexpressible factor of open intelligence blasts through intricate frameworks of ignorance about human sexuality. Open intelligence cherishes data as its potency of great pleasure and benefit. It is instinctively recognized that open intelligence provides increasing pleasure potency.

Shifting erotic events are the energy of potent open intelligence. A decision is made that there is nothing other than that. Human sexuality is open intelligence surging.

We know how to carry all erotic circumstances in the indestructible open intelligence vehicle. Open intelligence blows open confusion about human erotics, ending ignorance forever in the openness and spontaneous presence of pure pleasure in all circumstances. Free of confusion about human sexuality, open intelligence society initiates sane, healthy eroticism for the first time, disentangling it completely from social, religious, educational and personal injunctions that

attempt to control erotic conduct and rights by restricting it to the sexual domain and a list of do's and don'ts. Potent pleasure and benefit is not restricted to any particular set of experiences and is self-arising in all experience.

Through clear clarity discernment we question the datum of giving over our open intelligence potency to authority figures who have established all the do's and don'ts about pleasure identity. We're perfectly capable of establishing a beneficial open intelligence identity as the vantage of our incredible human society. We do not need to rely on old, unclear ideas.

Open intelligence, the fundamental identity of human society, is introduced at the point where the hologram of data is vanished, is done, and beneficial society manifests stable, super-clear, spontaneously ethical, skillful, naturally fulfilling beneficial intent. In open intelligence, benefit, prosperity and generosity are the prime and only directive. Human society's collective intelligence is the resounding strength of individual and total society, maintaining its blissful fabric and potency, without any effort, without anything needing to be done.

The potency of open intelligence normalizes all data, befriending them in ordinary, everyday love and benefit. Now this alone, open intelligence, which is the definition of each of these words, frees us from the constant hum-drum of belief in cause and effect related to data. Thus, everything whatsoever changes within experience. It is completely cleared up that our well-being is not related to any kind of cause and effect relationship of our data streams. All ideas about cause and effect as the basis of our well-being are subsumed; the idea that one datum will bring us happiness and well-being and another one won't, or that a healthy body will bring us well-being and an unhealthy body won't is seen through. Thoroughly cutting the root of all beliefs about our well-being, establishing complete well-being in every single moment of the here-and-now, no matter what the old ideas describe it to be. So essential, so simple.

This current moment of open intelligence—that's it. No words to understand here or memorize, nothing at all to do—open intelligence alone. The only purpose of any of these words is to elicit open intelligence, subsuming cause and effect. Don't try to get it down. To even try to understand or memorize it is not necessary. Open intelligence tells all. It shows all in every moment, showing that whatever those labels are of the old programs, they are completely uninstalled already by the very nature of who you are, no matter what the struggle has been in trying to describe yourself or your individual identity, to make sense of it, to get it down so that you will be someone right here.

Where is that past identity? Show it to me right here if you have it. You can't do it. And what about all those horrific or wonderful projections about the future. Where are they? Blown open, always, without anything needing to be done—pleasure blowing everything open without anything needing to be done.

Day Nine Talk

Different people have different data streams about their bodies. We can't say that there is anyone else who has the same data that we do, so in a certain sense that makes us very unique. We have that sense of special, precious uniqueness, but at the same time we're extensive, which means that any kind of intelligence that is represented in nature is very definitely represented in each one of us. In every single one of our data is a statement of nature itself. So, that's really marvelous, you could even say miraculous.

If we come together with another person, then it's a matter of mutual allowance and mutual respect. If we're clear about our own data, then that really lets us connect with other people. We are an open-source for all data, and only through knowing ourselves in that way can we really know other people and where they're at.

We reach a moment of knowing that, whatever we're feeling or whatever our experience is, that is representative of the experience of countless beings who are having exactly the same experience at the exact moment. We really feel open connectivity with everyone, where it isn't any longer so much about *my* stuff. When that is clear, we really get into a flow of giving and receiving that is inseparable. In society we've pretty much trained ourselves to focus on our own stuff, or if we've trained ourselves to focus on each other, the focusing on each other is often very secondary to focusing on ourselves.

Next we see, wow, it's not just us and our data streams—everyone else has exactly the same dynamic going on. It doesn't matter who they are—president of a country or homeless person or anyone in between—every single being has exactly the same dynamic: open intelligence and data appearing in, of, as and through open intelligence.. That's very humbling and yet so connecting, because what's seemed so complex and out of control suddenly makes sense in a simple way.

One of the great beauties of open intelligence is that it allows spontaneity. First of all it allows the spontaneity of self-knowledge, really knowing ourselves as we are and relaxing about it. Whatever our data are, they start to flow in a relaxed way; they're not such a big deal anymore. That alone is a tremendous boon, and it comes from the introduction to open intelligence.

We're not so indescribable after all. We can really understand ourselves deeply and readily, and it doesn't require a lot of specialized help and lots of learning. It's very simple and very direct and can be taught to anyone. This is very important. These are the basics of totally open intimacy.

By the power of open intelligence we have a kind of amnesia about our past suffering: "Oh, what was that really like?" The door has been completely shut and it is impossible to ever go back to that place of complete ignorance of open intelligence. That's truly tremendous because it shows us individually what can happen for all of society. It shows that we can shut that door and walk away, and over time the memory of that past suffering will become obsolete. We give up our primitive ways of being, and we can see that our other approaches to understanding the human dynamic have been really primitive and unnecessarily complicated.

These primitive patterns were something I recognized in myself. Even though I had worked on these patterns for years and years in very intensive settings, at most their impact was merely lessened, but never removed completely. However, by relying on open intelligence, psychological patterns are completely gone beyond, and the impact of the whole of society completely ending patterns—where they no longer return in experience at all—is extremely noteworthy. That kind of command of the human experience gives us a power that we have never had before.

A lot of the strategies we have had up until now have been so vague and also so totally interwoven with psychology, psychiatry, religion and spirituality that there is no way to really establish where these ideas began, what their current state is or where they could go. If someone looks for help with their emotional patterns, there are so many different things one could do, but there is really nothing that can ensure a result of complete mental and emotional stability—until now.

In the process of evolution we discover how to make ourselves stronger and how to adapt to our situation. It's the process of natural selection: we adapt for the species to thrive when it gets into trouble, and so this is where we currently are.

TRUE INTIMACY AND CONNECTIVITY

Today many people are very connected with the news media and can follow what is going on all over the world. This hasn't always been the case. Some years ago it took a long time to get the news, but now we live in a world that is really open and connected. We can really see the intensity of human society, and now through the Internet we can see our own and everyone else's data. Until the inception of the Internet it was generally only a matter of our data and those we knew or read about, but now we can see everyone's data online. For whatever data there is, we can find people who affiliate with that same data.

This is actually a great display of openness, and this same kind of openness is required in each of us as individuals. This is what openness provides: true intimacy and connectivity through knowing ourselves. At first it seems like a personal project, as if it only applied to us, but by the power of open intelligence, without even contriving anything, we start to feel really connected and truly intimate. However, it's not a contrived intimacy, like when you're sitting around in a circle with talking sticks and letting it all hang out. "Now it's my turn to talk; this is what happened to me." These types of methods may be a move in the right direction and they show that we want to connect and to belong and affiliate, but true intimacy and connectivity come through the power of open intelligence.

To really thrive we need to have a basic sense of ourselves— then there's no great mystery anymore. If something challenging comes up in us, we know exactly what to do. There isn't so much a sense that something could take us down. In the past we might have worried about a return of such and such a state, but now we have a sense of mastery and sovereignty over our own condition. This is very, very powerful, because this sovereignty is an expression of our resilience and our ability to thrive in all situations and circumstances.

Your ability to thrive is the model for everyone thriving, and not only that, it's the exact explanatory model of how everything survives in indivisibility. You are yourself an authentic expression of how everything whatsoever thrives in indivisibility. These could just be a bunch of philosophical words; however, if they're true in your own experience, then they're an experiential reality expressed in your own existence. Everyone becomes the zenith type of philosopher—not the sort of philosopher who has the intellectual head-trip going on, but the one who deeply and intimately realizes what they are talking about in their own experience. This is really fortunate.

CLEAR INTELLIGENCE

I have been talking about erotics and the erotic nature—the anticipation of pleasure, what will bring pleasure, the ideas we have about that pleasure, the ideas we have about where pleasure comes from. What one sees is that pleasure is the basis of all of our experience, and it's only the *idea* that things are otherwise that has made it seem that pleasure isn't the basis of all of our experience.

No one is a victim of the circumstances or ideologies they have adopted, and furthermore, no one has sovereignty or authority over the way you describe your own experience. The idea that pleasure is restricted to the sexual domain or that the erotic of human nature is limited to the sexual domain is just an unfounded ideology that was fabricated out of all kinds of religious and philosophical ideas.

When we are introduced to open intelligence we see immediately that the sexual domain is not the only source of pleasure, and we also see that positive thoughts, emotions, sensations or experience are not the only domain of pleasure. *Everything* is the domain of pleasure. In fact, to get to the ultimate pleasure, it is required that this self-arising natural pleasure be actually experienced in negative states. This subsumes all the ideologies we've learned which say that pleasure is restricted to the sexual domain. According to these ideologies the twinges and urges that we have are called "sexual," and we come to believe that they have an independent nature. We come to believe that they can drive us and control us and that they are signs that we must do certain things, like hook up with someone or have a child or whatever the ideas are.

All these ideologies have been created by someone, but none of them have authority over anyone. It's up to each person to find their own erotic domain and their own sense of pleasure. It's up to each person to take care of themselves in a way that derives pleasure from life. What I am referring to is not some kind of corny idea of pleasure, but the basic, simple pleasure of sovereignty—the sovereignty that every individual has in their own experience: their own innate dignity and integrity that don't need to be regulated by anyone else.

Things have gotten very confused, to the point where many things are regulated that shouldn't be. Natural parts of human experience are regulated within justice and legal systems and within institutional systems like medicine and psychiatry. We need to see that these things, while they may be helpful in some regards, don't really represent a basic understanding of our experience. We need to look at ourselves as we are and then decide what our laws are going to be, rather than hauling in these outmoded legal structures that try to control everything we do.

When human society doesn't allow reproductive rights to be an individual right, then that is very significant. Something is very, very wrong when people lose their right to decide what they can and cannot do with their bodies. We need to take the power into our hands and decide clearly from a very clear intelligence how society is going to direct its pleasure potency to take care of everyone.

We find within ourselves that our basic open intelligence can carry us through in all ways, that it can provide everything we need, showing what we need and how to get it in a beneficial way. It shows how to get even the most basic of needs—food, clothing, shelter—things that we generally think we have to work for. We no longer feel that we need to devote our entire life to the accumulation of money in order to have security and comfort. Instead, we need to see where that security and comfort really come from. Only from our open intelligence are we able to act in a truly beneficial way. The commitment to this alone is worth an entire lifetime. It is absolutely the best way anyone could spend their life.

It is a complete priority. I made it a priority in my own life, and I am very happy that I did. I had many choices, but the results from the commitment I made early on in my life couldn't be better. It may not look like all the scripts that were written for my life; however, the script that unfolded is a damn good one, and everything in it has come from the priority to open intelligence.

Throughout my life I was very lucky because I didn't just meet one kind of person; I met all kinds of people living all kinds of ways. I was a little Catholic girl, the eldest of six children, living in the 1940s and 50s, and my parents were very open-minded. One of the adults I knew then was a friend of my parents, and she was a gay woman. She had the same birthday as mine, so I felt we had a very special bond, and she would always make it a point to connect with me on my birthday. She was dean of students at the University of California, so she was a very accomplished woman. She never said anything to me about her lifestyle, but through her example and through the examples of others, I knew that there were many choices about the expression of sexuality and that it didn't have to look any one particular way.

The basis of how we express ourselves sexually can only be grounded in open intelligence. If we want to have satisfying sexual experiences, the focus needs to go into open intelligence, rather than into the actual sexual experience. The ground and the foundation in that experience is open intelligence.

In the process of getting to know ourselves sexually, a lot of us were told that it's not okay to touch our genitals. When you were little your parents probably removed your hands from your genitals whenever you touched them, or maybe your parents didn't do that because they read somewhere that they didn't have to do that, but still, automatically and spontaneously all over the world people grab their kids' hands from their genitals. That basically says, "Don't touch yourself there." I'm talking about these things because they're very engrained in society, and they're very engrained in each one of us.

The whole process of getting comfortable with yourself and knowing yourself really requires that you be freely allowed to touch yourself if you choose, so go ahead. Even if it feels uncomfortable at first, just allow it to be and see how that is. You can call it anything you want—self-pleasure, self-sex, masturbation—but most important of all is to know that it's okay. We want to learn this ourselves, and we want simple nurturing of healthy sexuality to be part of the way human beings function.

GAINING CERTAINTY IN OPEN INTELLIGENCE

We want as well to have a basic understanding that there are a lot of thoughts, emotions, sensations that come up and that they are all just data appearing in our very clear intelligence. They have no power or influence, because they have no nature independent of open intelligence. Without open intelligence, they wouldn't be; all their juice comes from it.

It's entirely up to us what you do with these things. No named thing can drive you to do anything in any particular way. Even if someone else forces you physically to do something you do not want to do, you still have complete sovereignty over your stability in that event. We see all kinds of people all over the world forced to do things they do not want to do, and maybe at some point you've been forced to do something you didn't want to do, sexually or otherwise, but at all times you have complete sovereignty of open intelligence in that situation.

There are great cultures like the one in Tibet, where there has been a strong practice of open intelligence for a long time, but Tibet has suffered devastating consequences because of invasion, war and the destruction of much of their culture. I have many friends in Tibet who had to flee an invading army; they started out with hundreds of other people, but maybe only a few survived the journey. They went through incredible obstacles like people shooting at them from the air and from the ground, but what did they say about that? They said, "My experience was that it increased my confidence in open intelligence." They could have had endless stories rolling this way and that way, but their primary take-away was increased confidence in open intelligence. This is a very compelling example.

I can say the same thing about my own life: the big take-away in life is increased certainty in open intelligence—the absolute assurance of open intelligence. To me that's the hallmark of a successful life. We all owe that to ourselves; it really is the priority. I hope that if it isn't your priority that it will be, because no matter what you think you know about the world and no matter how accomplished you are, open intelligence will show you a lot more about any of that than you ever dreamt you knew. It really does subsume all notions of everything.

THE DOMAIN OF PLEASURE

When we are raised believing that we are faulty, that we have shortcomings and character defects that we will never overcome and that we are pathological creatures, then we really need the sovereignty of open intelligence to challenge that. You cannot mix open intelligence practice with micromanaging data. Open intelligence shines forth from within all data, and the assurance of that comes about through short moments—or just hanging out! If you just hung out for a few years with other people who are gaining confidence in open intelligence and never practiced short moments, open intelligence would still dawn. It dawns like all the crazy notions had dawned in the past: because we hung out with the crazy notions and gave them some space. We previously said to all our data, "I'm all yours!" but now, instead, we hang out with open intelligence and give it some space.

Our data no longer have power and influence. For example, if someone looks at you the wrong way and that ruins your day, then that's just up to you. They could then do something else, and if your day is ruined by that, once again, it's totally up to you. We can each stand strong in our own open intelligence, and no one can take that away from us. By empowering that strength in ourselves we become very clearheaded and our whole body is radiant. We can physically see the difference in ourselves, and other people might also see it in us. "Wow! What happened to you? You look different. You look more relaxed." When someone says something like that, they're just recognizing themselves in you. "Wow! I am seeing myself for the first time. If someone else can be like that, I can be, too."

Opening up the domain of pleasure and the domain of erotic experience to include everything is so grounding and stabilizing and is such a great release. It's like having a big bathtub filled with murky water, and you take the plug out and all the murky water drains away. All the murky ideas are completely gone forever, and we don't even care where they went.

By relying on open intelligence, data is clarified forever. We ground ourselves in a basic intelligence that is real and which really allows us to connect with ourselves. If we just spent our whole life connecting with ourselves in that real way, that would be enough. Your own contribution of this moment of open intelligence is so entirely beneficial and healing to everyone. It's the act of a great warrior, a great hero.

Just by practicing open intelligence, it clears up all kinds of patterns of data. This isn't just true for you. When, by the power of open intelligence all these data are cleared up so that it never returns, that loosens the hold of all these confused ideas over society. It is very, very powerful and complete.

It is a transition from thinking ourselves to be pathological, flawed creatures who have been cast out of the domain of pleasure due to bad behavior. We see ourselves instead as we really are, and we're not being cast out of anywhere. Our pleasure domain is right here—in whatever our current experience is.

Your circumstances, whatever they are, are the support of open intelligence itself. No matter where you are, here or there, it's entirely up to you whether you choose to have open intelligence as your basis. You have complete dominion over how you want to live your life, no matter what you've created before. So, that's a good starting point.

Open intelligence is always the ground; it's always the foundation. It does not matter what other people are doing. They become your helpers, constantly reminding you; they're all friends in their own way. Somebody gives you a dirty look or somebody gives you a kind cuddle or anything in between, and it's all the same to you. This is the proper attitude. You are a warrior of open intelligence.

If somebody marching out of Tibet being shot at from the air and from the ground can rely on open intelligence, so can you. This is a good example. You can see clearly, "Oh, wow, there are other people just like me who can rely on open intelligence, no matter what the circumstances are." There are people everywhere who can live in their circumstances and see those circumstances as supports.

It doesn't matter where you live or what you're up to: all data are circumstantial; now this one is appearing, now that one is appearing and who knows what the next one will be. A series of thoughts may come: "Oh, I've got a neurosis. I've got a thought disorder. I'm a weirdo. This thing has a power that's going to get me. It's controlling me," but these are data that are following one after the other.

It's something that is really good about all data is that they only come one at a time. Even if we see all these data coming at us, what can we say about it? We pick something out and see it as one thing coming at a time. Nothing is overwhelming; it is just one datum at a time. What could be simpler than that? One datum shining with open intelligence at a time.

REAL OPENNESS

The ability to really have always-on open intelligence is directly connected to our data streams about our parents. This is pointed out very clearly in the Empowerments, where there is a very thoroughgoing clarification of data as regards our parents or early caregivers.

In order to be able to love and to have a healthy adult relationship, it is required that we completely cut through and blow open all our data about our parents. All of us have all kinds of ideas about our parents or caregivers. Those range in degree, so we've all either had ambivalence or outright hatred towards our parents or early caregivers. In recent decades it's become popular to blame our parents for all the data we have now. In the light of open intelligence we get to love our parents, regardless of their data. And how do we do that? By loving *ourselves* through relying on open intelligence.

When data about our parents come up, it is not an opportunity to criticize them. If we think we cannot help ourselves at all and we will just go out of control if even the thought of our parents should arise, then we need the support of our trainer and we need it immediately.

It doesn't matter who our parents are or what they did or what happened afterwards, and this recognition is extremely essential to our own well-being; otherwise, we will drive ourselves crazy with all these data streams. Being at ease with these streams is deeply connected with our ability to be open and present in adult relationship, and this is the reason that they're addressed in the Empowerments. All of these ideas are happening right now; there isn't any past available anywhere. If they are going on about parents or anyone else, the negativity, chaos and confusion are happening *right here and now*. This is very, very important to recognize.

Hatred is hatred by any name, so we need to confront it directly and extract the power of love; we blow open the power of love that is the essence of hatred. How do we do that? Not by ignoring hatred, but by encountering all of our negative datum openly.

Here we have a safe way to do that, not a way that is going to encourage us into a chaotic expression of hatred about parents or anyone else. There is a real openness with everything we actually feel and with everything we actually think.

No matter how cut-off or weird our parents or early caregivers were, they're human just like us. They're ruled by the same data that are present in all of human culture. How sad and difficult! What a torture that people could be ruled by this.

EXTRACTING THE SELF-ARISING POWER FROM HATRED

Anyone's expression of ambivalence or hatred towards any group reflects on everyone. We need to face it all and avoid nothing. This is absolutely key. When as an adult we have an intimate relationship with someone, we will want to really be open with all these data from our childhood—everything, avoiding nothing, extracting the essence of self-arising bliss and not letting any data be a secret hideout for anger or resentment. In every short moment of open intelligence we have an opportunity to cut through all hatred of every kind, to overcome it completely and to extract its true power and essence.

Even though we may recoil at our own hatred, it's important to let it be exactly *as it is*, and this is true of any of these very charged states. That allows us to draw out the love-fury and our true ability to love that come out of hatred. It is not a separate thing from hatred; it comes out of hatred. It is extracting the true essence—the self-arising power and bliss—from hatred.

There is no need to recoil, but even in recoiling, let it be *as it is*. We realize how much human beings have the ability to hate. Whatever our big, charged states are: anger, hatred, jealousy, pride, arrogance, ignorance, and all the other things that we don't like to think we are, we just let it be *as it is*.

We all have these feelings. We all share them alike, because we're all part of the same culture, and we see them encouraged actively. A big display of it comes in all our news media: one negative datum after another, after another. An excellent opportunity to practice open intelligence is to just watch cable news!

In open intelligence we can tap into being completely open and really connecting in deep feeling and in true compassion, not some kind of made up, cultivated compassion. We connect with true compassion and connection based on getting into the depths of our own negative states.

People come up to me sometimes and they say, "Oh, I'm having so many data come up; I feel so negative." Good! I'm not going to encourage you to sit there and wallow in every negative thing that you have and all its associations. We both know the solution, and we have a way to share that and to clear it up forever. This is very, very powerful. If there weren't a way to clear it up, then it would be scary.

If you are facing all those horrible things that happened in the past, rely on open intelligence—steadfast, strong, straight up, indestructible. It is the indestructible essence self-arising in each of these powerful states. The states have no independent nature. Extract the power right here. It isn't anywhere else; it's not over some distant horizon. It's right here in your horrific state, whatever it is—the more horrific, the better!

No cop outs required. You know what a cop out is? An antidote or a curative fantasy. "Oh, can't have that thought, better go over here and have these other thoughts." All of them are equally the power of open intelligence. Connect, connect, connect—open connectivity, straight, strong and steadfast.

Value Letters from Participants

FIRST SHARE

I have seen sex as having a great power over me. This sensation I called desire was a burden and something I would preferred to be without as I saw that it dictated my actions and wasted hours, days and months—either rejecting it or desperately chasing after it. I was told often to beware of this thing called sexual desire, that a young man can get himself into a great deal of trouble if he is not careful.

So indeed I did find myself in troubling circumstances, mostly in the realm of intimate relationships, in what seemed to be an endless cycle of falling in love and falling out of love. When I was not in an intimate relationship I desired that one special person; when I was in a relationship, I desired everyone *but* that special one.

The Four Mainstays have given me the ability to see how much energy I was dispersing chasing after these mirages. I feel now far too lazy to take on the old stresses I associated with sex and intimate relationships! I can now simply and naturally relate to people without those old expectations ruling my actions.

I walk around this wonderful community of people and feel so fulfilled with intimacy. I am in awe of how a knot I thought was so massive came undone without my really doing anything but be supported. What a joy and freedom this is to not have to spend my life as a victim to my urges and surges.

SECOND SHARE

Wow! I think you just cleared up everything I have ever been confused about: self-arising bliss in this moment *as it is*. Yes, I have heard it before, but this time it struck me even deeper—the open intelligence blast blowing everything open in unending open intelligence.

What I learned to be the sources of pleasure was eating sugar, being in a happy intimate relationship with the greatest sex life, sleeping, traveling, rush experiences, drinking alcohol, partying.

Well, of course, it never gave me complete pleasure, and so the search continued.

I learned that erotic urges and surges needed to be acted on, and if they weren't, the relationship wasn't good enough, which always brought me a lot of despair. I believed that I or the other person needed to change (mostly the other person) or that the relationship needed to be changed or ended. I thought that erotic urges and surges were only appropriate in the context of an intimate relationship and otherwise needed to be well hidden.

The Four Mainstays together with today's training have shown me that, when I allow erotic urges to be as they are, there is full connection with my innate beneficial power. By being at ease with the impulse to search for pleasure in something outside myself and not acting on it, there is a self-releasing power to be of true benefit to myself and others.

There had been a lot of confusion for me around intimate relationships and sexual desire, but my trainer has been of great support when it comes to relying on open intelligence with these very strong impulses. She gave me very straightforward and practical advice, leaving me free to act from and enjoy open intelligence instead of hoping to get something in the future.

Today's training has been totally eye opening. I really love hearing about puberty and how this totally confusing time in life can be one of fully recognizing the great power to be of benefit. Because I work with students this age, it is very clarifying to hear what puberty is all about—this time in life when everything seems to be turned upside down.

Being around the community has shown me how these erotic thoughts and feelings can just flow right on by. I have seen that desires don't need to be either avoided or indulged. More and more I have been able to relax with what is here, seeing it for what it is, instead of believing that something needs to change. It's been very relaxing and potent to see how this plays out in daily life.

Instinctive open intelligence has opened up my view, releasing happiness and more and more energy and beneficial power into my life. Less and less do I get involved in stories about getting pleasure, now or in the future. This choice makes me free to choose in a responsible, powerful and truly connective way.

This has been the most powerful day of my life. Candice, endless thanks for showing me how to live as an optimal human being. It is a power that I knew we all had, but never seemed to be able to figure out how to release. All my love and endless thanks.

THIRD SHARE

For me, I never felt love in the way I thought I needed it, and in turn I felt incapable of loving, as I wasn't sure what it really was. I was role-modeled that love is conditional and in some ways it was something earned that could be handed out and taken away. The words were spoken, "I love you," but they rang very hollow. Intimacy was very much tied to sexual partnering. It, too, felt contrived and judged.

After the birth of my first child, when she was placed on my chest, I touched into what I knew was the closest expression to love and intimacy I had ever felt. While it was directed towards her specifically, there was the sensing that this sense of love and intimacy filled the room and that it was beyond me, and indeed totally unconditional and not tangible at all.

As I remain steeped in the Four Mainstays I am reminded of the truth of that experience. True love and intimacy is not situational; it is the juice of all situations. Love and intimacy are the shine of open intelligence. This is demonstrated in my life through the everyday ordinariness of really seeing people, of truly listening, of an openheartedness that allows for the inclusion of everyone, of the desire to help others, of asking what is needed and acting upon that, of giving a helping hand, of asking "How are you?" and really wanting to know, of saying "hello" and "thank you" to people who previously went unnoticed, of knowing you don't need to "know" someone to feel a love connection.

Intimacy is in the sameness and oneness of everything. It is the fundamental basis and root of connection we all share. It is not bound up anywhere; rather, it is shared freely in all data. It is the key that unlocks the shackles of a burdened and confused mind, and its twin is love. Thank you for so graciously and humorously showing us this naked truth. With deep respect and gratitude and, of course, love.

Day Ten

OPEN INTELLIGENCE SOCIETY

The Written Text and Commentary

Please, take this advice: Rely on the Four Mainstays—short moments of open intelligence, the trainer, the training and the community. In this way, the great open intelligence identity is increasingly obvious. Very simple and direct, no fooling around.

In very great open intelligence society, all afflictive circumstances are increasingly outshone by each individual's powerful commitment to a single short moment of open intelligence. Moment-by-moment, society and the individual are increasingly stable and beneficial. Do not underestimate the incredible potency of the single short moment of open intelligence. The Four Mainstays support complete 100% assurance of open intelligence 24/7, without any hideouts.

The open intelligence view and data are inseparable, indivisible. Instinctive recognition of open intelligence unleashes profound intelligence that is not available in relying on the descriptions of data.

Countless, ceaseless and unpredictable data arise; however, open intelligence is reliable and stable, regardless of descriptions of the here-and-now. Truly real open intelligence is very stable identity right here. It has no fantasy life. It is stable and beneficial in the current moment without reference to frameworks. It is known by its super-benefit of total sanity and stability that is recognizable throughout all data, private or public. Due to its indestructible, unchanging na-

ture, open intelligence has no need to spin out into descriptive frameworks. True open intelligence is recognized by its inexhaustible benefit right here, individually and collectively.

Make no mistake about it, open intelligence is recognized in its obvious benefit. In open intelligence, all responsibilities and commitments to others are honored. If a change in relationship is needed, it is carried out in a respectful and highly beneficial fashion, honoring everyone completely. Open intelligence is not an excuse for irresponsible hurtful behavior. Out of control disharmonious behavior indicates the need for the Four Mainstays; it does not indicate stable clarity. Never be confused about this. Open intelligence is all-beneficial and solution-oriented, displaying benefit, prosperity and generosity right here. That's in there because I had some questions that people asked about that. "Well, if open intelligence is in everything, it's okay if I'm unfaithful to my partner even though I promised to be faithful. In infidelity, open intelligence is present." That may be true; however, do you want to live like that? We get to see clearly what's going on, and open intelligence is not an excuse to just act in any way we want, even though there's been a mistaken notion about that these days. Open intelligence equals benefit. There's no open intelligence separate from benefit, and the benefit is right here; it's right here in your own stability.

The trainer is of enormous support. They have successfully benefited from open intelligence in many life circumstances. They completely understand where you are at.

Everything is outshone in open intelligence—the potent pure luminosity of beneficial qualities and activities. All the various strategies, actions and methods of data are subsumed in the beneficial qualities and activities of clarity-intelligence. The most comprehensive order is clarity-intelligence evident in sprawling, free-wheeling spontaneous beneficial qualities and activities. The ability to spontaneously benefit your own here-and-now, no matter what its name is. Total stability right here.

Hey!—open intelligence normalizes all data, so there is no need for fantasy worlds or elaborations of any kind. Everyday open intelligence is where it's at. Waking, sleeping, making love, defecating, working, eating—whatever—open intelligence is where it's at. Hey!—this short moment of simple, radical open intelligence right here is the means to link in to current open intelligence. Press the button, again and again, until open intelligence is obviously continuous! That just means you're stable, completely stable at all times. It's obvious with no need to rely on open intelligence, just obvious at all times. Increasingly it's clear that open intelligence has always been obvious, even when it wasn't recognized. Even in non-recognition of open intelligence there is clear recognition of open intelligence and that's when we all break out laughing! That game we've been playing called "non-recognition of open intelligence" is fueled by open intelligence!

Shining forth spontaneously and effortlessly, the intrinsic intelligence of each datum expands into open intelligence instead of endless stories. Open intelligence is a world of always increasing spontaneous benefit, prosperity and generosity, pervading all of life and reality, equally and evenly. The consistent ongoing fulfillment of beneficial intent is society's powerful momentum. In each short moment of open intelligence, humans seal the beneficial nature of current and future society.

Conventional identity offers no result of complete mental and emotional stability. There is no map leading to that goal. The Four Mainstays provide the comprehensive map showing the powerful skillful means, open intelligence right here, for increasingly beneficial, prosperous, generous society individually and collectively, as well as stable and powerful identity. Yeah! Open intelligence identity is where it's at.

Once open intelligence is confirmed as your own nature, it quickly takes over as the only fundamental identity. It just makes simple sense. Right here, no brainwork required. Its wondrous ride offers peak pleasure increasingly, putting a permanent smile on each face and assured ease in each stride.

In one short moment of open intelligence, self-loathing and all related data are understood and released, opening truly powerful, beneficial identity that outshines all current data, all past data and all future data; what I didn't do, what I'm going to do, stable right here. Data have no hold and are like space. Space is ungraspable. Similarly, data are ungraspable. Where are they now?

Humans have been living in a fantasy world of descriptions which validate a strictly causal reality in which it is impossible to have complete mental and emotional stability. This cause and effect fantasy world is like a hologram or a mirage and is a primitive existence when compared to open intelligence, which provides complete mental and emotional stability right here, inexhaustible benefit right here and complete solutions right here in all situations. As society evolves due to open intelligence, many current ways of living become obsolete. This moment is unimaginably stable when lived from clarity-intelligence. Just a point to make here: you can see all your own data as a society of data. You can see how all these data become totally stable in yourself, no matter what they are. So the individual and also with society—so, the collective society, just like that.

In open intelligence's greatly expansive all-beneficial nature, the beneficial energy once focused only on relatives and friends and oneself opens up to include everyone. What a relief! Don't have to put it just in one container anymore. Can let it flood out everywhere. Our generous display of beneficial qualities and activities for all in this short moment is the very best connection we can have with our loved ones, as it offers the power of example of a human being endowed with clarity intelligence. This is the greatest contribution we can make to our loved ones and to society. Each short moment of open intelligence sharply accelerates our own benefit and the benefit of all.

Hey! Open intelligence blows open all data into clarity-intelligence. When data is expanded by open intelligence, a new intelligence comes about for us as individuals and for human society, one that is inaccessible when relying on current data as an end in itself. Open intelligence takes everything in at once; it has an all-embracing, beneficial, direct knowledge that sees the nature of everything. No kidding, no fooling. A boon of benefit, prosperity and generosity opens up in this moment of unending open intelligence! The here-and-now is where everyone is at, filled with benefit, filled with stability, right here!

The greatest addiction of society is belief in the independent nature, power and influence of data. Believing that data have their own nature, power and influence independent of open intelligence is the only addiction. Open intelligence outshines the need to roll out stories about data as though they have an independent nature, as though they have an independent nature to fuel your well-being or not. Totally stable right here, regardless of data. Open intelligence offers profoundly beneficial solutions right now, to me, to you and you and you and you. For example, open intelligence has the power to do away with a lifetime of disturbing emotional patterns. Wow!

Open intelligence is indestructible, unchanging and unending naturalization of the great high sought in any datum, including alcohol and other substances. By the power of truly real open intelligence, it is impossible to be addicted to any datum.

Relying on open intelligence rather than addiction to data is a real boon of truly real sanity that brings bright perspective and a balanced view. Open intelligence outshines the impulse to elaborate data into pleasant or unpleasant stories, and open intelligence is right here, always stable in each here-and-now, with no special data associated with stable identity.

As superb open intelligence and its treasures dawn, assurance is obvious, and data are outshone. Its luminosity shines brightly within each here-and-now. In open intelligence, everyone profits at all times in one way or another.

Hey! All data are outshone by lively open intelligence. Instinctive comprehension of open intelligence unleashes super-potent power and intelligence. Very simple, right here. Your own stability right now, sensing everything, sensing your own presence. The total power of stable intelligence, nowhere else. Just like this, you receive the spontaneous empowerment of perpetual power to live beneficially. Open intelligence is inseparable from the superb stability which is the benefit, prosperity and generosity of each here-and-now.

Day Ten Talk

Open intelligence devours all causal thinking, such as, "What about positive and what about negative?" This is a very important breakthrough to make: to break through to the spontaneity of whatever is present in every datum.

The written text goes into this fact in quite a bit of detail: data have a certain intelligence and open intelligence has a certain intelligence, and they're two very distinct intelligences; yet, they are *inseparable*. That can never be figured out within causal frameworks.

It's very natural for people to say, "Well, if everything is equal, then what about all the hideous things that occur," or "What about these pleasant experiences that are all mine." Rather than lessening all of experience, open intelligence heightens it. If there's a feeling of total despair about the world and the condition of human society, open intelligence exponentially heightens that. It becomes not only a matter of one's own despair, but it encompasses all despair of *everyone*. To encompass all the despair of everyone would be completely overwhelming from reified intelligence, because we can barely incorporate our own despair, but by the power of open intelligence everything is encompassed.

Even though from the data view it might seem like the best you could get would be the neutralization of negative experiences, that isn't what occurs at all. All data are heightened to the max and burst open into open intelligence. The key is that open intelligence is inseparable from the experience; the open intelligence and data are inseparable and indivisible. The tendency to go this way and that to try to figure things out is completely overturned. This stability opens an all-at-once type of intelligence that incorporates everything, sees everything and knows how to move forward in all circumstances from the vantage of indivisible open intelligence.

This continues to go on and on: being able to have freedom in the immediacy of the perception of the absolute futility of the datum. There is a whole new way of looking at life that is very bold and brave, very strengthening and not neutralizing at all.

Neutralization is the whole activity of avoiding the flow of data or replacing one datum with another datum. Open intelligence clarifies all data as to their true nature. We don't just wake up to pleasant data; we get to wake up in *all* data.

WARMING THE HERE-AND-NOW
WITH OPEN INTELLIGENCE

When we live from data, no matter how brilliant those data are, if they don't include open intelligence, it is really only a fantasy world. There are not any sets of data that are more privileged, more sane or more insane than any other sets of data. By the power of open intelligence we get to be right here—not darting to the past or into the future, but right here, exactly as we are.

Although this transition can be uncomfortable at first because it is unfamiliar, it quickly opens up into pure pleasure. This is not pleasure that is some kind of imagined conceptual framework for pleasure; rather, it is the pure pleasure of instinctively recognizing everything exactly *as it is*. There is the complete knowledge that there is nowhere to go, that there is never an escape from the here-and-now. It is so simple.

We only have four ways to deal with data: indulge them with all kinds of stories of this and that and the other thing; avoid them by saying, "No, I don't want what's happening here and now;" replacing them, "Oh, this here-and-now I don't like, and I want a better one, so I'm going to put some new dresses on it and see if it looks better," and then lastly, to clarify them, which means to warm the here-and-now with open intelligence presence.

A situation may not look like what we wanted it to look like or what we thought it would look like; nevertheless, by the power of 100% commitment, increasingly the reality we see and experience is just so much more likeable, so real and vivid and not in need of any props.

When people who are committed to open intelligence come together, they know where the other committed people are coming from; they know that they have not come together to try to get a date or hook up or get involved with the mixed motives that are usually floating around when lots of people get together. Instead, everyone knows the score, and that creates an incredible space of safety and comfort. Because it is a safe and comfortable environment, it is reasonable and logical that all kinds of data would then come up, but it's the best place to let all those things just hang out.

If we're looking for a certain pleasant set of experiences, then it may not look quite the way you expect it to be, but by relying on open intelligence, a more likeable reality is created right here and now. Thinking about the future is still here and now. This is one of the interesting things we get to see: it's always the here-and–now, even when we are thinking about the future!

THE TRANSITION TO OPEN INTELLIGENCE

The transition from relying on reified intelligence to open intelligence can happen quickly or slowly, and while for most people it happens slowly, there might be quantum leaps here and there. But whichever it is, we become more and more familiar with open intelligence and adjusted to it. As we do so, our plans and activities don't have so much stress and tension in them, until the stress and tension disappear completely. It's similar to when you make a new friend: it usually takes a while to grow in trust with that friend, and it is the same way with open intelligence decision-making. We grow in trust with the spontaneity of open intelligence, and we grow in trust with its laser-like decision-making capabilities and ability to apply the correct solution in the moment.

With two years of complete commitment you see the fruits; you can see how far you've come, and because of that you can trust yourself, and you can trust open intelligence to know that this process will continue to unfold moment-to-moment. So again, it's very simple. The simplicity is so totally reassuring because open intelligence prepares us for any eventuality. We grow more and more secure, even to the point of knowing, "Well, death could come at any moment. No matter what that might entail for me, I'm ready."

We're simple, we're direct. Here and now is where it's at; complete stability here and now, that's where everybody is at. It doesn't matter what name it has attached to it—complete stability is where it's at. There is no way to get out of the complete stability right here, nothing that can be said about it that would make it unstable. By the power of relying on open intelligence, the whole fantasy world of data is subsumed by open intelligence, right here and now.

Things play out how ever they do, and how ever they play out, you're totally stable and secure. In this way you've made the best investment in your future, in your personal life and in your business life that you can possibly make.

All of us have our own circumstantial data. You could think of it like a constellation of data. We have our own constellation of data of the way we've identified reality that makes us, we hope, feel safe. But we find that no matter how many data we get in our constellation or how much we try to make it stable and positive, it never quite is. In fact, it so much *isn't* stable. In the total stability of where we are, right here and now, we find all we need. That's all we can count on. No matter how many other factors we've put into play, it all comes down to right here and now. This is where we are at. The flow of data is natural and circumstantial. Whatever your data are, open intelligence is the key.

ACKNOWLEDGING WHO WE REALLY ARE

With a strong datum like shame, for example, it could be fixed into a box through applying a method to it, and if it's fixed into a box, then it'll be neutralized or tamed, like teaching a dog to sit. But the minute you turn your back and you are not taming it anymore, it will jump up. That's the key distinction between clarifying shame and merely avoiding shame or replacing shame with another datum. In clarifying shame, it is allowed to be *as it is*, and in that it is recognized that the shame is about not acknowledging who we really are—thinking that we're overcome with character defects and shortcomings, that we need some kind of remote power to fix us and that maybe that will happen sometime in the future.

In open intelligence-strength we find that this supposedly re-mote power is *right here*. It's in the shame itself; the power is arising within the shame. We don't have to neutralize the shame by avoiding it or replacing it with something else. It may sound paradoxical, but that is our true strength, and it's right here. If you have been interested in cultivating conscious contact with a higher power, you find that that higher power is *right here*, al-ways indivisible from you, and the conscious contact is 100%. You can call it conscious contact, but it is right here and it is indivisible from you—100% right here and now. That is the real power to serve, to be with everything exactly *as it is*, not need-ing to hope for some future day when it would be corrected—finding the power in it right here.

This is what real sobriety and sanity are: not being afraid of anything. It's possible to get just as drunk on shame as it is on alcohol or other drugs. The great addiction is to data and all their labels. We can get high in our own way on data—shame or anger or whatever we want to call it. Whatever your data are, *that* is open intelligence. The demonstration of that is responsi-bility in the here-and-now—being right here and now, totally present and clear, without needing to hold on to any frame-works.

In dealing with what most of society would call a severe men-tal disturbance, the solution is the same. There are already people who are teaching patients who are institutionalized to maintain open intelligence. To do so really helps a lot, regard-less of the situation. No matter who we are, at some point we'll really get out there with all our data, and open intelligence right here is always the key.

There is a lot of confusion about who is mentally challenged and who isn't. We see from open intelligence that the line be-tween "sanity" and "insanity" isn't really so defined. We can see that however anybody is acting out, wow, we've been there too in our own way: seeing things that weren't there, imagining things, acting totally crazy, or whatever it might be.

Whatever our safe little world is that we've built, by the pow-er of open intelligence right here, we are totally stable. In data all kinds of alternate realities can be created, and some are socially acceptable, some aren't. In open intelligence, right here, we get to see all-embracing knowledge of all worlds right here; it's not going to be anywhere else. We don't need any sort of alternate reality.

FILLED WITH BEAUTIFUL CONNECTION AND CARING

I've been married for a long time, and every single day I marvel at the depth of what that means and just the simple ordinary connection that is so unlike every fantasy I could have ever had about married life—but so infinitely more likable, so rich with total treasure and total, beautiful connection and caring.

I can remember as a young mother feeling like I didn't know what to do with my children. Here I was all of a sudden with this little human being in front of me; I was totally in love, but I still had no idea what to do. I'd learned everything I could about good role modeling, and all of that did nothing for me, because it always came down to a moment-to-moment interaction.

I became overwhelmed with the need to be a perfect mother, and I would say that this was one of my most afflictive states. It was forty years ago, in the early days of books about parenting, and I was reading every single one of those books. However, it always boiled down to moment-to-moment interaction: what was going to happen in that moment, and what would best inform that interaction? I am so glad the great mother open intelligence took care of it all; otherwise, I would have been a real busybody, I'm sure! Through the complete assurance of my own open intelligence, I was able to see the open intelligence potential in my children and to know that as their ground. I saw that they are completely responsible for recognizing their own open intelligence and that I could not do that for them.

Whatever our interactions are, the whole process of living boils down to the here-and-now. If I had come to those situations with my children with a lot of expectations of what they should be, then those expectations could have easily been dashed. However, if I come to the here-and-now with open intelligence, then my expectation is always confirmed. Open intelligence—no need to think about it. Simple, ordinary, direct, enhancing all relationships here and now—this is where we're at. We're never anywhere other than that, and that's true for everyone, whether they're a loved one or not.

For everyone the soothe-ability of each moment is open intelligence. That's the ability to thrive; that's the resilience in every single datum. Open intelligence, self-arising from within each datum, is not a band-aid to be applied to data. Band-aids fall off, but open intelligence is inseparable—warming all data just like sunlight warms the air. It warms all kinds of air—cold air, hot air and all air in between. It rests on everything equally.

There's no rush, just the here-and-now whatever it is. It bursts open all data, whatever they are—positive, negative or neutral—but in that bursting open we get to see everything clearly. That's good. It's the only way to go.

Value Letters from Participants

The first job I ever had was as a dishwasher in a busy restaurant. I worked for many hours in a kitchen full of stress and alcoholic chefs. I enjoyed the solitude of the dishwashing machine, as I could avoid contact with most everyone, get the job done and leave.

And so now, about eight years later, I have resumed my dishwashing career here at the Center in Sweden! But now I can see the simple, clear distinction between a society based on data and one focused on open intelligence. I look forward to my time washing the dishes here, just being around people who are completely enjoying work that is on one level quite mundane. There is absolute effortlessness all around as the task at hand is skillfully and joyfully carried out.

I had lots of data the first week of being here at the Center: "I hope no one yells at me for doing it wrong," along with a natural urge in me to hide out in a corner to avoid interactions. These data ultimately just played themselves out, as I was surrounded by appreciative smiles on all sides. All the activities I saw around me in the kitchen and all around this community were exalted with open intelligence. There were lots of people busy getting the job done, and there were no personal games, sexual tension, gossip or any trivialities. Working and being with this community gives me complete conviction that relating in this wonderful way can also occur in society as a whole.

Because of my old ideas about things, I still have this notion that I am under a microscope and that surely these horrible raging thoughts I have will set off some alarm bell and they will come and kick me out. But the fact that these thoughts can come and go without my being bothered is evidence of the power of the Four Mainstays for me. The louder, more abrupt and pervasive these thoughts are—jealousy, sexual desire, endless life planning, needs and wants for recognition and fulfillment—the more I see that the support works.

As the text said, "Open intelligence normalizes all viewpoints," so there is no need for fantasy worlds or elaborations of any kind. Everyday open intelligence is where it's at. Thank you so much for this text, Candice; every sentence is a true work of art. What a relief. I can leave all the mirages behind and be incredibly powerful and spontaneous, completely ordinary, totally present in each amazing moment, energized and of benefit.

SECOND SHARE

Thank you for these unerring instructions that are bringing about an optimally functioning human society. This is so exciting and humbling. A society based on data is very limited because of outdated and non-workable models. A basic misunderstanding that assumes that humans are fundamentally flawed and powerless has cultivated a society of oppression, aggression, fear and dis-ease. However, it seems like we've reached a turning point and we won't stand for this mode of living any longer.

An open intelligence society is forming throughout the globe. In open intelligence society the core competence of open intelligence is everyone's common agreement, and what a difference this makes! People are working together for satisfaction rather than credit. Generosity replaces greed and hoarding. Cooperation, harmony and empowerment of everyone are becoming a daily standard. Everyone takes responsibility for their data, giving up the right to be a victim and to take hostages. Engaging in gossip, criticism and judgment is not even thinkable and is replaced by warmth and a deep caring.

I am completely grateful to my mentor and many trainers for their unwavering guidance, love and support. Through their steadfast example, I have been able to resolve strong data, and I've become the person I always wanted to be! The training is a constant companion, enriching my life with powerfully potent instructions that take hold both intellectually and instinctually. They've increased my ability to speak confidently about the way things actually are. The community makes for a fun life. I love our open intelligence campus here in Sweden; there are so many shining examples of optimal human beings here—people totally onboard for global change. This is the way I thought life could be anyway. What a gift.

Open intelligence benefits my everyday life in all areas. My thinking has become focused and clear and disturbing stories are not a distraction. My body becomes more and more relaxed even though I'm busier than ever. I am developing many skills, like managing teams and projects, and I've learned so much about media and web technology. There is no longer a focus on what can't be done, but rather the drive to find solutions, knowing that one is just around the corner. I'm really enjoying a new-found flexibility in collaboration, with where to live in the world, and where and how to spend money.

I increasingly feel a deep connection with many people and I'm no longer driven by competition and fear. I think I just feel okay with everything *as it is*, not looking to some future destination of a better here-and-now. Each here-and-now grows brighter and brighter. Thank you, Candice, for illuminating such a beneficial way of life for everyone. In love, respect, gratitude and service.

THIRD SHARE

Today I am so grateful to be the child of my mother and father.

The love I feel for them is merged with the pain I feel in seeing them struggle with data. I never really honored my father in my life, but in the last two years we have had more intimate contact than ever, and we can enjoy each other more and more. In a way I see him more at rest with things than before, with a willingness to look clearly at his life.

I deeply wish for my mother to be at rest with herself. The unrest I was confronted with my whole life from her has been— and I am sorry to say it like this—a pain in the ass for me. Now it is a pain in my heart knowing her to be so at un-ease with herself. I always wanted to change her into this compassionate, warm mother, but my trying to change her made the situation even worse, of course.

Now, the pain I felt is replaced by love. There is nothing I can do and nothing to make her change her attitude towards the viewpoints she has. That is the most challenging thing I can see in front of me, right now, right here, but I can rest with the pain—mine and hers. And love her.

Having full support of the Four Mainstays has been of immense value. My teacher so lovingly gives me the opportunity to rest with my viewpoints as they are, and he reminds me again and again that I can choose open intelligence-identity rather than data. The trainings are meaningful beyond speech, going into the heart of open intelligence, always.

Candice, I want to thank you so much for making it known to me that I can be there in the most beneficial way for my father and my mother when they are in need. I know now, though I want to learn a lot more about it, that being of benefit to all is just one short moment away, and every time I take it, it is enough.

Day Eleven

THE FEROCITY OF OPEN INTELLIGENCE

The Written Text and Commentary

Belief in the independent nature of data is frozen and stiff, a freezing hell, regardless of name tag. It doesn't matter what you call it. **Fantasies—intellectual, religious, psychological and so forth, depicting no possibility of immediate potent stability—are gravely in error. The solution is this moment of open intelligence. This is the future utopia people are looking for as well as the extinction that is feared;** both at once, simultaneously. **The introduction to open intelligence gives us a clear view of reality, right on the spot. Unending open intelligence is obviously an unbroken sequence of instants.** No way to grok that, to get your head around it with logical or conceptual frameworks. It can only be instinctively recognized. Instinctive means "does not need thought or reason."

Clarity society is lively and potent, fierce and openhearted, right now, fearlessly outshining individual and collective data from within, blowing open individual and collective fantasies in the bright beneficial power of current qualities and activities.

"Open intelligence" means overall openhearted, fierce potency—the mode of openhearted, fierce potency and knowing that is required for entirely beneficial qualities and activities. That's what open intelligence is. The first moment of open intelligence may seem like, "Oh, wow!" or "No big deal," but by the power of short, uncontrived moments, fierce potency becomes extremely expansive, increasingly expansive, potent, warming up everything without exception. It is an openhearted fierce potency, and not some cut off state.

A short moment of open intelligence shines longer and longer, brighter and brighter, without any need to do anything special to increase its length or brightness. Short moments, short moments, short moments, everything opening. This is another way of saying, training up potency is the fierce blowing open of all data in the here-and-now, leaving no trace, like a supernova exploding with such exponential force that no trace of Earth or any other dimension is left remaining, not even a single memory, only the force and potency of open intelligence shines brightly in all dimensions, providing inexhaustible benefit endlessly in all directions.

Similarly, a short moment of open intelligence is like a supernova—potency outshining data. By the power of this, all confusion is subsumed in potent open intelligence, qualities and activities, right here, in the current moment. The initial short moment is the first moment of 100% assurance and stability that is engineered into the indivisibility of the multiverse itself, each short moment, 100% assurance, 100% stability. How ever many worlds may or may not appear, all whatsoever are subsumed in the sovereignty of indivisibility and potent clarity intelligence. This sovereignty, indivisibility and potency is what open intelligence is—a completely fierce openheartedness without limit.

Open intelligence potency is true identity—identity that is multi-modal. It can assume countless, ceaseless, unpredictable, all-beneficial, wonderfully powerful identities. Open intelligence always assumes beneficial identities. Open intelligence never misinterprets the nature of data. Open intelligence never misinterprets the nature of data, ever.

This is another way of saying that a person who has open intelligence does not merely dwell in cut-off open intelligence, but partakes of human existence in openhearted, fierce benefit to all.

Thus, the inseparability or indivisibility of open intelligence luminosity and its fierce, openheartedness surges as the super-factual dynamic energy of everyone, blowing them open and out of whom they take themselves to be into clarity potency. All those ideas about who we are, so restricted, limited and confined—blown open, blown open completely, delightfully. Never too much, delightfully.

Open intelligence is the mode of fierce potency that occurs in this instant of open intelligence. The term here refers to the fact that open intelligence takes everything in at once; it has an all-beneficial, decisive knowledge that blows away conventional knowledge, booting up potent knowledge that pervades all viewpoints across all dimensions and worlds— personal and collective. "Collective" here means all multi- versal dimensions, known and unknown to humans. Who knows; all we have is the here-and-now.

Reified intelligence on the other hand knows one thing at a time or accumulates data and draws associations among them; it has a "this versus that," indirect, divided knowledge. Thus, the meaning here is that open intelligence, because it is decisive knowledge of the fundamental nature of all data, knows everything in its fierce, decisive mode right now, rather than in the mode of indirect, indecisive, wimpy reified intelligence, which is like a cat watching a mouse and toying with it. You know how sometimes initially it might be, "Oh, open intelligence is the witness," and then the data are over here. It's open intelligence watching the data, like a cat watching a mouse; however, it is just another datum arising, in this case of "the witness." Again, by the power of open intelligence, all data are outshone like sunlight filling space.

In other words, open intelligence has certainty and complete assurance about the nature of the current datum, as well as all data whatsoever. Not just intellectual comprehension, but complete groking, complete getting it. That's what instinctive means. Instinctive, without thinking about it, to the point where the display of beneficial qualities and activities is what is obvious, is what its demonstration is.

Similarly, without thinking about it, space has complete assurance and certainty of its potent stability pervading all appearances. Space doesn't have to think about it, "Oh, am I pervading planet Earth? What about the Milky Way, am I pervading that? What about that other dimension in Star Trek. How am I doing there? And what about the bardo or the hell realms or the karma or the sin or whatever it is? How am I doing there; am I pervading there?" Space pervades everything instinctively, without thinking about it. Its indivisible, unavoidable bind is paramount. Its beneficial activities of holding everything together perfectly, without any effort, without anything needing to be done—that's what is absolute and demonstrated, qualities and activities, the unavoidable bind.

Clarity-viewing is the seal of the clarity view within the current datum; that's open intelligence viewing, open intelligence, **like the indivisible potent force of space pervades everything within it. Open intelligence liberates the conventional definition of the current datum.** I'm so glad!

Open intelligence also liberates any conventional definition of open intelligence itself as some kind of datum restricted to certain positive data, such as a breakthrough insight, a special realm, or another collection of certain data. Together and inseparable, open intelligence and the current datum outshine conventional reified intelligence in open intelligence, a more comprehensive order of potent human intelligence, an unbroken sequence of human instants of superknowledge and beneficial society extending throughout all dimensions. That's the way it is.

Day Eleven Talk

The special state we're looking for is right here and now; it's never anywhere else. So, that's good to know! Real open intelligence has potency and liveliness, and without liveliness there is no open intelligence. Its ferocity is built into this moment. It isn't at some future moment. The ferocity of beneficial qualities and activities is right here. The big boom of the voice and the power of the body of open intelligence are all right here, indivisible.

For example, for a performing artist of any kind, in order to really be able to connect with an audience, it requires coming from that place of totally open intelligence. The self-consciousness most people feel on stage or with a microphone in their hand is a situation that is perfect to warm up with the fire of open intelligence. In that instantaneous datum of nervousness, there are all kinds of data that can come up. "They're all looking at me. Everybody wants me to sing just for them. Am I going to say and do the right thing?" Part of becoming a great performing artist is letting all of that be *as it is*. It is not a matter of trying to get rid of the afflictive states, but using the afflictive states for the power and the potency of the performance.

Open intelligence is the ideal voice training for a singer or for anyone else, for that matter. In singing about open intelligence or doing any kind of performance, it is essential that the actual aspects of open intelligence be represented. Otherwise, no matter what is stated about open intelligence, the statement will be pointing to something other than open intelligence.

THE FULL FORCE OF OPEN INTELLIGENCE

These days there are many mistaken ideas about awareness, clarity or open intelligence. People often see it as a special state that they want to escape into, but it's very important to not make any mistake about the potency of open intelligence. It isn't some washed up, wimpy, wiped out state. It is a fierce potency which explodes all ideas we've ever had about anything—about ourselves or anything else. So, this is very helpful.

The body, speech, mind, qualities and activities of open intelligence are already fully instantiated in this moment. They're engineered in. By relaxing we find we're extremely powerful. We might initially think, "Oh I'm going to be a couch potato if I rest naturally; I'm just going to veg out," but we find something much different about ourselves.

All of us have read all kinds of things about, clarity, awareness, open intelligence or whatever it might be called; however, when things are read or heard that truly point to open intelligence, then boom! *BOOM!* No more kidding around! The hammer is brought down; it's absolutely clear. This is the song of open intelligence. It's not some kind of messing around or marginalized state for people who live some much different way than any of us. This is really important to communicate.

The special state of fierce power is right here. It's in the current moment, whatever that current moment is presenting for you. It might be a panic attack, it might be the thought, "I'll never make it. Where am I going to get the money to pay the rent next month? Oh, wait, what about that girl over there; wow, she looks good." It could be anything, but whatever the thought may be, that's where the power is; that's the special state we've been looking for.

Wherever you go, there you are, and that's where open intelligence potency is—the full force and power of open intelligence ferocity, not needing to go anywhere else to get it or to demonstrate it in some future time or remembering some past time when it was demonstrated and now it isn't. All the games are over. No matter what the presentation is, here and now it is a presentation of the full force of the body, speech, mind, qualities and activities of open intelligence.

EXPANSIVE INTELLIGENCE

Open intelligence leadership naturally includes tremendous responsibility. It is a responsibility that comes from total self–responsibility for all of one's own data. Open intelligence training is not merely a matter of passing information from one person to another. It's full-on engagement by knowing oneself so

195

thoroughly and completely and being able to lead oneself so thoroughly and completely through the power of open intelligence. Having maturity in that equals maturity in leadership. If we are in a leadership role and we don't know what to do with our own afflictive states, then what are we going to do with our team when they start losing the focus on open intelligence? Real leadership is the absolute call to open intelligence in oneself.

We have a lot of ideas that float around in every moment, but open intelligence clarifies and vastly expands all of them. Our intelligence no longer feels restricted to this body alone. We can actually start to decisively experience in each moment that our intelligence is open and vast and is not limited to a body. Our intelligence is beyond anything that we can imagine or reference. Just letting that be *as it is*, we are the instantiation of that power right here. It may seem particularized in a certain way; however, it never is. It's never just here, and this is the meaning of indivisible.

There needs to be a common language to describe open intelligence, and not just a common language, but a piercing language that cuts through all the bullshit. Human beings want to be connected. We're pack animals, and we want to feel united. We want to know how to transition successfully to the world we are creating right now. The way the world is shaping up right now is so far beyond our imagination, yet we transition to it successfully through the power of open intelligence. When open intelligence informs all of our science and technology, then we're truly expanding our intelligence. We're no longer living from the limiting view that human beings are some kind of special intelligence somewhere trying to connect with other intelligences somewhere else. We see that it's all co-extensive, right here.

As to all our ideas about putting human intelligence in machines, well, how can we possibly do that if we don't even know what human intelligence is? We have to deeply understand, completely comprehend, decisively experience and instinctively recognize open intelligence. It is already engineered in. In the same way that we have found simple ways to talk about the make-up of the time-space continuum—proton, neutron, electron, open intelligence needs to be named specifically and uniformly so that everyone can understand.

Each here-and-now creates greater amnesia about the former here-and-now. Our whole idea about our make-up, our whole way of living and how we use our intelligence is completely shifting. The body is no longer required for beneficial qualities and activities; we already see multi-modal identities emerging. Everyone can be as many identities as they want to be today, and we are no longer fixated on one single identity. We could be the anxious one, the scared one, the powerful one, and we could have a Facebook page related to each identity, and we could be tweeting about each persona.

It's always been like this really, but now we're growing into it, seeing who we are, seeing we're not as limited as we thought we were. The expansiveness of open intelligence is able to hit the mark. Each of us is engaged in different activities, and by the power of open intelligence in our skillful means we hit the mark. How do we learn to hit the mark in our skillful means? Through our own sets of data. There is no common set of certain kinds of data that everyone has to adopt. This is a great, great opening, beyond any other leap ever made by humankind. For a while we have thought of ourselves as the greatest intelligence on this planet, but that's going to change.

WARMING UP DATA

Open intelligence warms up all data in its openheartedness. It warms data up to a blazing temperature—an inferno even—so that they cannot exist any longer as they were. Data are outshone by open intelligence. The noticing of any states that arise requires no comment, or if there is a comment, so what? Having a comment is not some kind of final declaration of identity.

We all want to be mature and full-hearted, and that is right here in the warming of all our data. By the power of short moments, oh, that warmth gets in there! It's a simple, radical, revolutionary, fiery act. It may seem like, "Oh, so what?" at first, but believe me, there is power in you and power in short moments of open intelligence.

All the holding on to all the different data melts in the warmth of open intelligence. What a miracle that is! What an expression of total connection we are enacting! That connection is in each of us—in our own short, uncontrived moment where we recognize open intelligence. The power of short moment is beyond anything you could imagine. Just in your short moment, all of human society is changed forever. WOW! The new logic—weird, open and wild.

Value Letters from Participants

I am only 23 years old, but still life has been hard on me. Since I was little I have had big expectations of myself—from faultlessly cleaning my room every Sunday and making coffee for my father in just the right way when I was a child, to being the perfect girlfriend and skillful student when I grew older. I have constantly been trying to change myself into a better me, writing endless lists of what needed to be fixed. I never seemed to be able to live up to my own expectations. It went on for so long till I came to a point where I didn't even know if I loved myself anymore or if I was worthy of being alive.

One day my sister and I sat down in the sofa in our apartment and she told me she had found something. It was Balanced View. She introduced me so beautifully and I was just stunned. When I heard that I could be happy no matter what was going on, I thought it was too good to be true. Instantly I knew I had found something of great benefit and value.

One year later my past seems like a distant dream. Today my life is not at all like this, but at the same time so much is the same. I haven't written a list of what to change with me for a year, because I know now that I am perfect just as I am. I am actually happy, deeply happy for the first time in my life. I can honestly say that I love myself and that there is a big confidence within me without me trying it to make it be that way. All my relationships with my family, friends and boyfriend have totally changed. I didn't know that there could be so much uncontrived love and openness.

To get the answer to what the purpose of life is and always having the solution in every moment is very precious. I have seen my strengths, gifts and talents grow, and there is stability every day in my life. I am so happy to have my sister here with me on this journey. We have always been close but just before we met Balanced View we had started to drift apart. Now we are closer than ever. Thank you so much for everything. All my love and gratitude.

SECOND SHARE

How does open intelligence benefit my everyday life? Well, I really feel like right now I have the perfect circumstances for relying on open intelligence, and I think my relationship with my father is actually my most perfect circumstance. Right now I feel like I can't wait to go and see him, and I see all my data regarding him as being only open intelligence. I have so many descriptions that I decided were true about him very early on. He was a victim of his parents' data, and I was a victim of his data. But now I just want to run to him and shake him and say, "We were tricked! It's not at all the way we thought it was; it's so easy—you're not going to believe it!"

I want to blow open each here-and-now, seeing all the little nasty, ugly, makes-me-want-to-throw-up-data about him as open intelligence. Oh my god, it's so funny how my dad and I have believed in all these descriptions. We've been walking around feeling miserable, hateful, shameful, degraded, and each and every day finding so-called "proof" of our descriptions.

I feel the pain in all of my body—his pain as well as mine, but open intelligence is still with me. Life will be different from now on. No more looking away in the face of suffering, no more indulging it either, and no dead end if I do look away or indulge either. I want to give the gift of the realization of open intelligence to others, just like it's so beautifully been given to me.

THIRD SHARE

I'm sure the training today was written just for me, every word fueling a great fire of commitment in me. These texts are astounding: "This is the future utopia people are looking for, as well as the extinction that is feared." Wow! This sentence tears through what I take to be obstacles. It even tears through the profound insights, so tempting to dress up as something to savor. Right now, nothing to wait for, complete amnesia of all hope and fear.

My trainer has been totally invaluable to me. He so kindly and skillfully guided me to the doors of hell, making sure I had everything I needed to have the time of my life inside, and then threw me in! Every time I felt overwhelmed, he would remind me of just how powerful I am and that there was nothing to be afraid of. He lent me the potent courage to see that everything I feared so deeply was only an expression of my own power and potential. More than anything else the ferocity of this relationship is what has given me my confidence.

This morning I deeply felt this same loving support; thank you Candice, your words were so far beyond what I expected, teaching me to never expect anything, especially with you. What you've shown us here, what you've given every ounce of your being to, and what I've so personally and deeply received from you since the moment we met is beautiful beyond anything I could have imagined. And this is only the very, very beginning of something that has no end in sight. I am honored to be a part of this. These last few days have shaken me to the core and opened my eyes wide. I am at once humbled and empowered.

When I heard you read aloud the gratitude, admiration and love that you have for us all and that you are awed by our majesty and beauty, my eyes filled with tears. I respect you so much for what you've done Candice, and I'm deeply inspired.

My heart and eyes have opened to a space that I dared not believe was possible before now. I have been deeply touched by the responses from so many participants who came to me yesterday expressing how much they were moved by my singing, many of them in tears.

This issue with my throat and voice, although easy for me to bear over the past year, has been blown open. I thought this issue was too personal and only limited to me and too unimportant to even mention in the group, and that there were surely 140 other people who had far more important questions than mine. But by speaking about my issue and being able to receive your incredibly skilled response, people have been helped on infinite levels and have been lit up so brightly by the loving and masterful embrace of open intelligence.

What has also struck me deeply with this retreat is the power we have together, the power we already are. Last night some spontaneous dancing took place in the cafe, and as I stood at the side of the group, grooving gently and chatting with a friend, the intimacy I felt with everyone in the room almost melted me away. I was in the midst of an army of wisdom beings who live entirely from the heart, who enjoy life in honor of its beauty and wonder, each person glowing in celebration of their existence as a unique part of the display of open intelligence. This is so infinitely more powerful than anything I've ever known or seen before—an irresistible force of people demonstrating what every human being knows is his or her potential. Open intelligence society is right here, and it is unstoppable.

Day Twelve

COMPLETE IDENTITY

The Written Text

"Identity" is an expression used throughout social sciences to imply the specification of person, to deliberately appropriate certain identities to an individual. Like actors on a stage, we read a script, memorize it and then act it. Nowadays, few humans know their user friendly identity; rather, they are acting out scripts with stories that have many ups, downs and confusions. Without straight talk, how can we possibly comprehend our strengths, gifts and talents or share them with the world.

We each share a basic identity available through the Four Mainstays. It will give us everything we need to lead a happy, fulfilled, well-educated life in which we can be of benefit to all. Wow! This is a promise society has never been able to make before. What a momentous event!

It is very important to support each other as much as we can to grow straight, stable, assured and of benefit to others. We have to allow for the special smart people as much as we allow for those who are terribly challenged and who need help of other kinds. Balanced View and Great Freedom help us with all these things.

Each here-and-now has worth and a consistent, indestructible measure. Each here-and-now has an absolute and relative ethical value that carries over for all entities in each indivisible instantiation of appearance or sound.

For each entity who realizes the primordial predicament, there is no data from which to view and simultaneous fundamental comprehension of all data. To multiversal society and each entity everywhere, this most basic of identity descriptions and solutions freely grants lifetimes of dignity, natural ethical accord, seamless interactivity and interoperability, potent benefit-giving, incomprehensible understanding and okay-ness.

The potent immediacy of the discovery of the actual value and measure of each moment provides the exact technology we need and its complement of specific instruction sets which are applicable to specific individual tasks of each person and their treasury of strengths, gifts and talents. The Four Mainstays provisioning of unparalleled breakthroughs to human education and intelligence increasingly brings unimaginable power, innovation and creation to the advancement of society, continuously unfolding an increasingly beneficial, prosperous and generous society in the current era and into the distant future.

That we have this knowledge and an unerring map that shows us each of our infinite aspects unmistakenly is a wish-fulfilling boon of exponential magnitude. The wish-fulfilling jewel includes all aspects, and all of its aspects must be available for humans to thrive. This is not a casual matter.

The most magnificent powers of basic identity can only be comprehended and instinctively recognized in your own experience, nowhere else. Open intelligence is the great normalizer and equalizer of all experience and is the greatest good fortune.

In open intelligence society, we each are royally blessed; we have access to pith knowledge that can never be changed, moved or taken away. Freely open to everyone, our global society quickly and surely clarifies a global clarity society. There is no other choice that we can bear to ponder.

The Four Mainstays' fundamental discovery has been made, detailed and recorded over decades, every nuance of its unveiling carefully recorded for all of posterity. Great Freedom and Balanced View provide the most supreme commando vehicle—the Four Mainstays—giving everyone everything that is needed to be empowered into beneficial society along with an unerring surefire method of introduction that hits the mark potently and completely. It removes all states of uncertainty, suffering and doubt, and there is an inconceivable advancement—one that has never before occurred or been accomplished, with the sort of precise fortitude and magnitude that would sweep the globe. Everything is in place; everything is given without error or mistake. The Mainstays are an indestructible vehicle in which it is impossible to stray into even one idea of mistaken understanding.

The Four Mainstays will support you to join in here to be of greatest benefit and can show you how to build a strong community wherever you live.

While we are friendly and available all over the world, we also are a sophisticated worldwide corporation and organization which is pioneering Internet technologies, telecommunications and science in many ways. We know how to take care of business and protect our organization for the benefit of all. This is one of our responsibilities.

As the atom was discovered along with its map of subatomic particles, the exact root structure of the fundamental identity of humans has been discovered, mapped, researched, applied and refined so as to bring absolute value to planet Earth and its inhabitants. We are so very happy to offer this discovery. Now it is up to Earth's inhabitants to put it into use, for it ensures complete accord among all inhabitants and the flourishing of all its life forms. It is as simple as that.

Simply train up in the Four Mainstays instruction set to attain beneficial knowledge that will greatly impact prosperous, generous society. In this brilliant open intelligence view that contains and understands all data, there is inconceivable beneficial knowledge and activities. Ensuring mental and emotional stability, it instantaneously pours out a wealth of strengths, gifts and talents.

Training up open intelligence through the Four Mainstays is the only solid basis for human society building potent knowledge. Everyone and everything—all phenomena of all kinds in all countless dimensions—rest indivisibly in nature's intelligence, which is expressed in open intelligence. Each moment of human intelligence is indelibly sealed by great perfection. The basis of human knowing and all actions is bound by this fundamental identity, intrinsic to everyone and everything.

Fundamental to all human knowledge is the crucial recognition of open intelligence—natural perfection—as the instinctive basis of all one's own experience. This knowledge is required for the transition that society is quickly making from an Earth and body-based society to a multiversal information society.

Effortlessly fueling the here-and-now, open intelligence is our complete identity and basis of each experience. The open intelligence of our own raw knowing gives vital evidence of natural perfection—alert and clear. This is the basic complete identity of human living that is the prime attractor. Open intelligence is alert and clear; it knows with its own way of knowing. Its own way of knowing clarifies all accumulated mistaken knowledge with tremendous ferocity and beneficial activity. Its raw knowing has no escape. Its alert, clear knowing sees through all knowledge with alertness. Open intelligence knows what is applicable to the current moment and what to set aside.

We need immediate benefit in human society, and it can only come from instinctive recognition of open intelligence as the basis of all our experience. By the power of that instinctive knowing, we have the basis for creating truly beneficial knowledge.

Open intelligence is the uniform basis of ethics and culture which provides the most wondrous complexity, as well as beneficial, prosperous and generous qualities and activities.

Day Twelve Talk

We each have responsibility for our physical boundaries and enforcing them. No matter who we are or where we live today, we can find resources to help us if we are being sexually harassed by someone else. Even if there have been a lot of things involved from the past and a lot of connection and attachment, it depends on what kind of connection you really want to have with the person now. You could begin by saying, "Hey, I want to tell you something. My experience is that this occurs, and I don't like it. Please stop immediately." This will have ripple effects of empowerment everywhere in the universe, and it will give you great security, safety and stability within yourself.

It depends on what kind of connection you want to maintain. How do you want to use the resources of your life? Do you want to continue trying to manage people who are offending your personal boundaries, or do you want to use your energy to connect with people who will support you in every conceivable way to be powerful and strong? Do you want to connect with people who respect you and give you the space to really shine with your strengths, gifts and talents? It's up to you. If there is a person who is harassing you in this way, then whatever he does, that's his thing. He has just as much of an opportunity to rely on open intelligence as you do, so it's up to him.

The words "forgiveness" or "forgive" are purposefully never used anywhere in any of the Balanced View training. It is difficult to have a clear idea about what a lot of these words mean at all, as we don't know their fundamental identity. All we know are elaborate afflictions associated with each one, and with each one it's impossible to establish the factors or variables associated with what that definition means. However, in indestructible natural perfection the value and measure is absolutely clear in each definition. Why not stay with that to inform the whole course of action? It makes it so easy.

If there are two quantities and one is known and proven and the other completely unknown and unproven, it's better to grow our intelligence from the absolute measures that also apply to all the relative measures. It can be talked about very precisely and logically, and it can be addressed with tremendous specificity that makes perfect logical sense.

HOW TO ADAPT AND THRIVE

With lots of these things, we've concocted a complete fantasy world about what our sensations mean. We have put into play a cognitive sorting process that has no rhyme or reason or valid basis whatsoever, and then we tend to think that we know it all. In some circles that would be called a severe state of delusion!

All of the very real everyday situations in our own lives are pervaded by indestructible natural perfection. So, we might as well let our "wanting to know about this and that situation" rest in natural perfection, and a course of action will be revealed which will be perfectly clear.

All of our ideas about everything are falling away. Twenty years ago some people said, "I'll never have a computer," or "Computers are bad," or "It's so disconnected to talk with people online," or whatever it might have been. However, now the widespread use of computers is the way we are going, so we might as well get used to that, and it is best to let that use be informed by the indestructible power of our own naturally perfect intelligence. Relying on open intelligence inevitably and unavoidably shows us how to adapt and thrive without any problem at all.

We know so much about the basic workings of the multiverse; we are a direct, explanatory, working and mathematical model of nature's intelligence. It makes perfect sense to apply the fundamentals that we know about nature to our own behavior. Protons, neutrons, electrons—positive, negative and neutral data—nothing different here than in all of nature. If we really want to have a true connection with nature that is open, interoperable and interactive and where we don't look at nature or the environment as a "thing," then open intelligence is where it's at.

All these problems that need to be solved, like for example finding forgiveness for someone, in this moment of indestructible natural perfection forgiveness is just a completely obsolete notion. It comes in the context of there being some cast of characters in some kind of drama where something needs to happen. Even if there is a drama going on and something needs to happen, are we going to scavenge around in our data to try to come up with a solution, or do we just show up—relieved, happy to be, knowing that in our own potency we'll be able to do whatever is required?

UNDERSTANDING THE ISSUE OF DEATH

As a society we need to understand the issue of death much better and get real about it. Today we have all these regulations and laws about what we can and cannot do with our bodies, but some countries that are more progressive in their thinking have a range of options for allowing people to end life if they want to. Suffering is the reason that most people choose to end their lives, whether they do so in volitional open intelligence or they do it out of such an erratic frenzy of data that they cannot go on. You can guarantee that suffering is coming to an end in your life by stamping your moments with open intelligence. That is the great act that creates an amnesia of suffering.

A BETTER WAY TO KNOW AND PERCEIVE

As a society our ways of helping each other are extremely limited and primitive, no matter what we may think of ourselves or our efforts. We can see that the results of everything that we think we know in general haven't worked out too well. We have the threat of mass terrorism, with which everyone in the world lives every single day, and this is the first time in human history this has ever occurred.

We have to see that we really need to do things differently. We need to really start to look at our basic way of knowing and perceiving and see if there is a better way to know and perceive. If there has ever been better ways for people to know and perceive, what are those better ways, and how can we use them to correct our course?

Throughout history there have been magnificent beings who were representative of open intelligence, and every single one of these beings used exactly the same tools. All of you magnificent beings have those same tools. No matter what happens—whether it's global warming to the point where we revert back to a hunter-gatherer society, or it is some kind of accelerated evolution that is required due to that challenge, or it's some other event—it's very likely that our intelligence will continue to expand in a way that is more and more bodiless. Through many, many different scientific and technological means the obsessive concerns we have had about the body and its sensations will grow increasingly obsolete.

Regardless of what happens—and that could be anything—open intelligence is where it's at. If we hear in this moment that there is a supernova that is going to blow us all to bits in twenty seconds, what are we going to do? How are we going to spend those twenty seconds? Flailing around in negativity or relying on open intelligence?

Depending on the variables involved, the prospect of death brings its own data streams. However, once you get into the hum of open intelligence, these great weights aren't so weighty any longer. They loosen up from inside; they're blown open into an intelligence that is resilient and which thrives in all situations, regardless of their descriptions.

No matter what we go through in life and death, we want to train up in here-and-now open intelligence—not anything else. There's nowhere to get to; that alone is a big relief! There is no special state to get to—just whatever is happening here and now. If we try to get into a special state, it will inevitably disappoint us. There will come a time when it falls apart completely. The seal of each here-and-now is indestructible natural perfection, and that can be counted on without fail.

As regards scientific advancement, technology and nanotechnology, we're progressing in a certain way that open intelligence is essential to those endeavors. If we're going to put human intelligence into machines, that effort needs to be informed by open intelligence. We already are putting human intelligence into machines. This whole room is filled with human intelligence put into different kinds of machines—extensions and expansions of our intelligence that we don't even think of as our intelligence. The lights, the fan, the microphone, the air conditioner, the MP3 player are all extensions and expansions of human intelligence.

The advancements in human intelligence will continue to sharply accelerate. If people replicate things that are sub-valuable in terms of benefitting everyone, then those will naturally be deselected from the process and the quality offerings will thrive. It's built into nature. We cannot go wrong; nature is indivisibly naturally perfect. Look at the mess all of humankind has created, yet here we are, completely confirming natural perfection. So, there's no way to get out of natural perfection.

For anyone who is completely relying on open intelligence, it would be impossible to simply go along with the regular data, because one knows the score. Not only that, there is so much support. Wow, I'm very, very happy for all of us. It's very, very good, because each of us can thrive together. We can support each other in really offering our strengths, gifts and talents directly from open intelligence rather than from micro-managing all the data.

THE TOTAL CONNECTION

The need to belong, to feel connected, to fit in, to love and be loved all seem to be a part of being a human being. This really raises the questions: what is real love and where does it come from? If we really want to fulfill those basic human drives to belong, to love and be loved, then we really need to know what love is in a very real way that applies to every here-and-now. Once we know that, things will be okay, and we will have the courage to persist.

Early on in my own life I had a totally instinctive recognition of natural perfection. It was totally real and more reliable than anything else I knew about. All around me I heard so many other things that were different from that recognition; however, I never listened. It doesn't matter what's going on; open intelligence can never be swayed. When I was young and I began my higher education, I showed up for college, and I didn't even last until Christmas. For example, in the physical education classes they wanted to teach the women the rules of football and baseball so that we would make better wives! But I went my own way, and over time I met people who really inspired me greatly, and I looked to what they had done with their lives, and I knew that I could do that too in my own way.

No matter what happens, we can persist in open intelligence. I had certain circumstantial data and my life was a certain way—just like I have circumstantial data now—but by the power of open intelligence we know what to do. We don't find love or our sense of belonging in delusion and fantasy lands. In open intelligence we find our sense of love and belonging and our actual strengths, gifts and talents that give ourselves and others a beneficial result. It's the core training and the most fundamental education. It is in fact the most advanced education; any other education that may be attained needs to be informed by open intelligence. Without open intelligence the education will be weak—a half measure or a partial solution that never delivers the goods.

All of us can live with a sense of belonging and total connection and commitment. All of us gathered here together are good friends; we have a real connection. I look at you or anyone else and I understand you completely. I look at myself, and I understand myself completely. That's what love and belonging are. Many people live their entire lives without having even one person that they have that belonging or connection with, nor will they have it within themselves. To know that connection in one's life is greatly fortunate.

The most basic questions we have about living and the most basic human longings are satisfied very directly right here in the complete identity that is fine with everything exactly *as it is*, which knows that that same okay-ness will apply in whatever comes up in any future here-and-now. Even if the sense of increase is very subtle and gradual; nevertheless, the increase will be obvious. In that way, every moment will be a miracle and a wonder, opening more connection, more love, more belonging, more skills and qualities, more activities that are truly of benefit to oneself and others.

Whether you're young or old it doesn't matter. If you are young, *wow*, you are so lucky. Those of us who are older, we look at you and think, "Wow, look at those young ones. They are so lucky, so strong and stable, *whew*! They are really ready to contribute to the world." Some of us have lived a long time and we've never seeing anything like this.

A SUPPORTIVE COMMUNITY

As regards all the doom and gloom scenarios that appear every day in the news media, none of that can actually make doom and gloom real unless you want it to be. The doom and gloom is totally up to us. It doesn't mean we go into some kind of fantasy world where there is no doom and gloom. It means that we greet doom and gloom directly *as it is*—indestructible and naturally perfect.

One of the things that I love about the Four Mainstays is that by using them we remain together and connected. No matter what comes up, we have a safety net; we have a sense of real safety and community together with people who understand us completely, and we really know it! In that we can place total trust. It isn't us alone off in our isolated place trying to make sense out of things but having no idea what to do with our doom and gloom when it comes up. We could try to apply a band-aid to our doom and gloom, but a band-aid would just fall off.

Instead of that we can connect with supportive community, and we know a helping hand is always available and a helping heart is right there. We no longer have the worry about trying to find security and then keeping it or trying to find the special one who is going to provide security and then splitting off with that special one into some kind of tiny cocoon to preserve the security. It all opens up much more easily and much better than we ever could have imagined while involved in seeking security.

All the different displays of the things that we can think up and we can do have never given us mental and emotional stability. Our intelligence is not worthy of the name if it will not give mental and emotional stability. Yet, we see in nature itself that no matter what goes on, it is indestructible and stable, indivisibly unified. There isn't anything within nature that has an independent cause. So, what does that say about us? The very intelligence by which we know is linked indivisibly to a seamless flow of nature's indestructible natural intelligence. We are never a cutoff little creature.

By the power of short moments we become acquainted with our solidity and stability through thick and thin. In open intelligence there is always knowledge of which action to take that will be of greatest benefit to all. When an action is of benefit to all, then it automatically includes everyone who is considered to be within that 'all': you, your family members and everyone else.

This insight naturally opens up the whole question of identity. "Who are we and what are we supposed to be? What are the presumptions and assumptions by which we must live? How much of the different factors that regulate our identity are absolutely necessary to survival? How necessary are things like gender identity to fundamental survival? What is at the core of survival?"

What is at the core of survival is of immediate benefit in this moment and is not something we need to get to in the future. What is at the core of survival is right here and it's indestructible, so from this indestructible identity we have much more latitude informing identity or identities. We can see from this indestructible identity right here that there are many kinds of beneficial aspects we can assume. For each of us as individuals it is of primary importance, and it is our prime imperative to know ourselves in this direct way. After getting familiar with that we can proceed more and more into the world and be of benefit to others.

A supportive community is the perfect comfort zone to gain that familiarity and solidity. Just as you would go to a school to learn anything—carpentry, cooking or neuroscience—becoming familiar with open intelligence requires showing up for a certain period of time to become clear and complete and to know what you are doing. You then proceed forward in offering your skills in a beneficial way to others. How very, very important then is the commitment to our basic identity and what we will do to nurture that and allow it to flourish.

THE OPENNESS OF IDENTITY

The old ways of looking at identity are not such a concern anymore. When I was a young girl in the early 1950s, the world was very strictly divided into nations, and in Western culture white, Western ideas were privileged over all other ideas. They were considered to be the best ideas, and there was not much openness whatsoever to any other ideas. Within Western culture itself there were classes just as strict as any of the classes in European royalty or in caste systems in India. People were divided up into those who were good and those who just didn't make the grade.

In the time I've been alive the whole idea of identity has totally opened up. When I was young there were fairly strict gender roles and a person lived as a female or a male and adopted the roles specific to them. However, if you did not follow the prescribed gender roles, and you were to do something like have a same sex lover, it was cause for tremendous ostracism. Depending on what society you were in, if your skin color wasn't right, you were completely marginalized to an unbearable degree. Women were quite marginalized as regards the economic work force and denied freedom in terms of reproductive rights.

Now all of these notions of identity have greatly loosened, and they've opened up until we have the society we have today—the loosening up of national boundaries, the movement into a global culture and global identity, a movement on the Internet out of all the fixed frameworks of who we should be. We can be anything we want to be on the Internet—an avatar or something else that has never existed. This acquaintance period that we're having, where we are getting acquainted with what we can do with the malleability of identity, is a real turning point for all of society. Again, the body is not going to remain as a primary function of identity, and instead of that, other aspects of identity are going to be much more important.

215

Things that we can't even imagine today will quickly become possible, like the ability to have elective longevity—to decide how long one will live and in what form. What has happened in my lifetime and what is happening now is a tremendous shift in all of human civilization. Open intelligence allows a person to completely understand how data come about and resolve, so the need for a fixed identity or to be a certain way isn't as rigid as it once was. A person who is clear and who does not have any resistance is much more likely to be able to adapt to what's coming. If events were to take a particularly unethical direction, a person relying on open intelligence would know what to do and how to forcefully oppose the unethical circumstance.

This openness of identity is real intimacy. We can only find it right here—intimacy in this moment, which is the intimacy of open intelligence appearing as our own data. We've been trained to think about our data in a certain way: our bodies, our sensations, our thoughts, our emotions; however, in open intelligence we find that all those descriptions are superseded by something much clearer and more complete. This is a comprehensive order of intelligence, not just for us, but for all human beings, and the people who have chosen to thrive by understanding intelligence and identity completely are the pioneer adopters and adapters of an evolutionary process.

I really need to emphasize with everyone that open intelligence is the answer. By short moments of the power of open intelligence, unending open intelligence becomes obvious. When we're all mixed up in the data, we're always obsessively thinking about what we're thinking and what other people are thinking, as though we even knew what we're thinking. That takes a lot of work. By the power of open intelligence we give up that whole fantasy life. "What's this one thinking? What am I supposed to do? Oh dear, I better not do that because then they'll think this." By the power of open intelligence we just know.

ENJOYING PLEASURE IN EACH INSTANT

The sexual self-obsession of all of society today really is based on not understanding sensations. We've trained ourselves to interpret certain sensations and the whole zone of erotics as something that is perverse, but that is a perversion of what our erotic nature is. Our erotic nature is open, wild and free— enjoying pleasure in each instant. It is the font of indestructible wisdom and joy, the font of indestructible ethical action and total emotional stability.

So, what do we do with that as a society? We put it into ideas about what twitch or sensation we're having and how this means something about that one over there, or what twitch they might be having and how it relates to us. Aaahh! All of this sexual self-obsession is definitely going to go away, whether you rely on open intelligence or not—because you will get old! You'll be over the hill, and you probably won't be thinking about it much, and no one else will be thinking about you in terms of it, because in a sense you become invisible. The older you get the more everyone looks alike, men and women!

When I was a young woman I met some very radical women from Berkeley, California. I was very young, and they were all just turning sixty, and they were part of the radical lesbian movement. They had left their husbands, changed their names, become politicians, and one of them wrote a book called *Over the Hill*. She described the whole experience of being a woman in society who is aging and becoming increasingly invisible to all the attention through which she had identified herself. I'm sure there isn't a person hearing this who does not relate to what I'm saying.

Many of us gather our sense of identification by the attentions that other people pay to us, and we are so wrapped up in sexual attention. "Am I sexually attractive to this one or that one?" These thoughts come even if we have no plans whatsoever of ever having any kind of erotic intercourse with them.

Open intelligence is where it's at. If you are very open to people and they misinterpret your openness, that's their problem; you don't need to change. You may need to explain every now and then, but you do not need to change. Relax in yourself, and in this way you come to know where real pleasure is: it's within yourself.

Everything that's looked for in all these sexual associations is right here in the indivisibility of perfect, indestructible open intelligence and whatever is appearing—the perfect intercourse, the perfect union, the big erotic high that is being sought in so many ways. The here-and-now becomes increasingly the place of pleasure, giving one a very clear knowledge of what to do and how to act with everyone.

To become perfectly clear about this takes one out of that situation of being like a ping pong ball going back and forth, never knowing what's going on because this twist and twinge is leading this way and another one is leading that way. One minute you're thinking about a guy, the next a girl, the next a dog—you don't know what's going on! We all have the things about us in that regard we don't want anyone to know. We all do.

Open intelligence education is very important, so allow yourself to get totally grounded in that. Thoughts and ideas about what we want to do will come up. "Oh, I feel so free now; I could just have sex with everyone if I wanted to." Or, "How do I decide which one to enjoy erotic pleasure with, or which ones?" It's entirely up to you, but with any kind of involvement of this nature, it involves you and at least one other person. So right away from open intelligence you can see that there's a lot more involved than just satisfying yourself, and that's called wisdom.

All the flirtatious energy settles in to indestructibility. We don't need attention from others to give us worth; the worth comes from open intelligence and not from the attention others are paying to us. So, make no mistake about that. We naturally become much more cautious.

KNOWING WHICH MOUNTAIN TO CLIMB

What mountain do you want to climb? Knowing which mountains to climb is wisdom in action. I'll tell you a little story about that. I love this story! I have an incredible friend who is now deceased, a very, very powerful Tibetan man who was the head of a huge organization. He had to flee from Tibet and come to India. He had many, many people he was responsible for, and when he came from Tibet, many of the people who knew him there came to where he was in India. He lived there for a long time, never doing what anyone expected. First of all, where he lived was clean, meaning that there was no cow shit! That by itself should be considered a significant miracle in India. Not only that, he slept almost all the time.

Over the years of his living there with his community in India, a great phenomenon took place, and no one could understand it. Scientists came from all over the world to study it. The great phenomenon was that the Tibetan women were no longer having babies. No one could figure it out. "Oh, is it because they have birth control? Is it because they can get a job and support themselves?" But the real reason was that through wisdom these women knew which mountains they wanted to climb and which they did not want to climb. Open intelligence was running the show.

When you are totally relying on open intelligence, it's natural to feel totally settled and not fried by sexual concern. "What does this twinge mean, what does that? Should I act on it, should I not? What does it mean if I have this thought or that one?" That is severe self-obsession with one's own self-sensations and thoughts.

Again, if we want any kind of action to take place with any other being, we want it to come from open intelligence, and we want that partnership to be one pervaded by open intelligence. That has to be the prerequisite for it. Without that there's no sense in having a relationship. That is the advice I would give from my heart.

Even though we may feel wild and free, if we just follow our urges, it will involve them too, and they will have all their own data. It is very fragile territory. It is also an excellent place to practice wisdom, true mental and emotional stability and open intelligence which will not enter in to any terrain that might be harmful to another in any way.

So, with all of the games—the flirtation, the needing to be noticed through looking this way or that by which one has identified oneself—we need to be crystal clear in the moment. "What am I doing? Is this really how I want to identify myself? By whether or not I'm attracted to someone or they're attracted to me?" This is what open intelligence is. It's *real* intelligence with no bullshit. We get to see what real love is, and through that we're able to make good decisions.

The responsibility of open intelligence is our core responsibility to ourselves. It puts us right where it's at, so all of our involvement with what other people are thinking and doing becomes very solution-oriented and profound. We're not looking at people any longer as objects that we need to manipulate like we manipulate our own data. We stop needing to manipulate our own data, and we stop needing to manipulate others' data. We show up as a place of service, responsibility and benefit. It's so easy and fun!

We can still look attractive, that's fine, but it doesn't mean that we're doing it to get attention that we desperately need so that we can feel like we are somebody. This applies to all of us.

A SOCIETY OF UNIMAGINABLE BENEFIT

It is important especially in this day and age to know how to measure ethical value, and the absolute ethical value is in open intelligence. Why is that so? Because it provides for the benefit of all, without doing anything. Just by its nature it provides for the benefit of all. By stabilizing ourselves in open intelligence, from that place we're able to make decisions on what to do and what not to do. What action is going to be of the greatest benefit to all? We just know what to do. If we need to skillfully find a way to remove ourselves from situations we don't want to be in because we really deeply do not feel that it is of benefit to all, then we will be able to do that.

This is part of adaptation. All these old ways of doing things are being set aside. We are sharply accelerating our adaptation as a species that will quickly leave behind reified intelligence and create a society of unimaginable benefit, prosperity and generosity. All the old paradigms of decision-making are completely falling apart. How are decisions made in this new paradigm? The decision is made by each person who chooses to adapt to the perspective of open intelligence, and those that don't adapt will naturally be left behind. This is going to occur in a number of ways, but genetically we're going to select ourselves out of emotional and mental instability. The core decision-making process in every moment is open intelligence.

Right now this is a transition period, and we all have to make these decisions. I've had to make decisions like this too. Will I go along with the way everyone else is doing it or will I not? If I don't go along with what everyone else is doing, open intelligence provides the skillful means for handling that.

As a society we've never had a measure for ethical value, but now we do: the immediate benefit of open intelligence provides absolute ethical value in this moment of the here-and-now. That's how we know of the inherent benefit and we know of a stability that has never been known before en masse.

The doom and gloom scenarios are all based on reified intelligence. Things could very well happen according to the doom and gloom scenarios; however, as we can already see all over the world, people are adapting to a comprehensive order of open intelligence that really can solve the doom and gloom scenarios we've created from reified intelligence. The evidence is in all of us when we see that right here in our own indestructible intelligence we are able to erase patterns that had us by the throat before.

This transition may happen slowly or it may happen quickly. It may happen in quantum leaps: staying still for a while and then making a quantum leap, staying still again for a while and then making another quantum leap. It doesn't matter which it is; you are who you are, and you have lots of support for whoever you are. There is no one right way; each and every individual is honored and privileged.

I have worked all my life to make this dream come true, and with all my heart I thank you for supporting me along the way. I never would have made it without each of you. I have such deep gratitude, admiration and love for every single one of you and am thoroughly awed by your majesty and ability.

Value Letters from Participants

FIRST SHARE

The Four Mainstays—I love this term! I am a sailor, and I know well that without a mainstay the boat is sunk! The mainstays hold fast the mast and sails and are the core strength of the ship. They are the reassurance that, no matter what comes, the mast will not fall. The mainstay provides the unwavering solidity for the mast that allows for the storm to be harnessed and for the forceful forward motion to be extracted from the turmoil. The mainstays are a soothing comfort. As we sail effortlessly to landfall, we are whole, complete and utterly safe.

For me the Four Mainstays have been the opportunity to get uncomfortably and squeamishly naked, with all my flaws and failings on show. By allowing myself to be seen in this way by my trainers and by myself in open intelligence, I could see, and experientially realize, that there were no failings—only natural perfection, only benefit, again and again.

In a 100% commitment to total relationship with the Four Mainstays I was faced with the reality of who I am: wide-open open intelligence with nothing held back, no hiding out. All ideas of who I take myself to be or who I need to be to be safe are undone again and again. The impulses and habits to belittle and disempower myself and others are cut at their root. Stability, strength and open intelligence are left in their place.

I am not in the mood for bullshit any longer. I am not in the mood for any dillydallying around. I am not in the mood for putting up with the way things have been. I am not in the mood for complacency. I am not in the mood for accepting the consensus that a society built on lack and pathology is okay, or that it is okay to continue to put up with that and even contribute to it.

The "afflictive" states that appear generously pour out mountain-like stability, confidence and energy to do what needs to be done. It unequivocally directs me to the reality that I can only take responsibility for my data, and that I am absolutely capable of making a direct, clear statement of "only open intelligence" in all of my relationships and leadership roles.

This life is my responsibility. This is my carefree, playful life of relaxed open intelligence. My life. Choosing what I want. Nothing else.

I look at all the afflictive states I have experienced over the last three years, and I see that they have each fueled this fire in me, even when I did not feel like they were giving me anything but pain. Even when I felt I would have given anything—even my life—to rid myself of the grief, the sorrow, the loss, the black depression, the failure, the unworthiness, the arrogance, the pride, the fear, the sense of imprisonment, the fear of rejection, the need to do it right, the physical pain and the overwhelming desire and heartbreak. Each time I have relied on the solid Four Mainstays, and with their total support these seemingly ever-circling data have spun out, leaving confidence in their wake.

I now welcome my button pushers. Facing everything, avoiding nothing, I know so deeply that my afflictive states are giving generously to me again and again the opportunity to see things as they really are. When this is hard to see I know where to turn: my trustworthy teachers, my indestructible community, the teaching, and to the instinctive recognition of naturally present open intelligence—the rugged Four Mainstays uniting us all in great mutuality of only support, only love.

It is incredible how this reality is being made obvious to us all. We are being given the opportunity to let ourselves go wild, to let the covers be pulled, to give up trying to be someone or to have a life that looks like anything at all. In accepting this invitation we free ourselves from all ideas whatsoever. We stay with exactly what we are for a single, simple, unbounded moment, and we acknowledge ourselves. With all my love and life.

BALANCED VIEW
RESOURCES

If you would like to watch the videos from the Human Identity Summit, they are available at the Great Freedom web site: http://greatfreedom.org/humanidentity_more.html.

If you are interested in reading more value letters from the participants, they are available at the Great Freedom Forum: http://greatfreedom.org/forum/viewforum.php?f=252

There are many resources available for anyone who is interested in knowing more about the Balanced View Training. The main information source is the website: www.balancedview.org. Posted there are numerous public talks, videos and books, as well as a forum where people all over the world share their experience of relying on open intelligence in daily life. All video and audio talks are free and can be easily downloaded in mp4 and mp3 format.

Also listed on the website is a schedule of Balanced View trainings offered by trainers around the world. Venues range from face-to-face training and public open meetings, to trainings and meetings offered via tele-conference bridge.

The Four Mainstays support everyone interested in gaining confidence in open intelligence. When confidence is inspired by the Four Mainstays—1) short moments of open intelligence, 2) the trainer, 3) the training, and 4) the worldwide community—there is increasing recognition of open intelligence until it is continuous at all times. Then there is no longer the possibility of being fooled by appearances of data, not during life and not upon death.

For participants who wish to contribute to Balanced View, donations are gratefully accepted; however, all are welcome, regardless of ability to contribute.

www.ingramcontent.com/pod-product-compliance
Lightning Source LLC
Chambersburg PA
CBHW052037090426
42739CB00010B/1939